JACQUELINE GOODNOW, the author of *Children's Drawing*, has researched and taught at a variety of universities and research institutions in Australia and the United States, and is currently Professor in the School of Behavioural Sciences at Macquarie University in Sydney. She has published widely in the general field of cognitive development and was co-author, with Jerome Bruner and Austin, of the influential *A Study of Thinking*.

The editors of *The Developing Child*

JEROME BRUNER helped found the Center for Cognitive Studies at Harvard in 1960, and served there as Director until 1972. He is currently Watts Professor of Psychology at the University of Oxford and Fellow of Wolfson College, Oxford. He has long been interested in the nature of perception, thought, learning and language, and has published widely on these topics. At present he is focusing his research on the early development of language in infants and on the role of the preschool in early child developemnt.

MICHAEL COLE is Director of the Laboratory of Comparative Human Cognition, at the Rockefeller University in New York. Trained initially as a psychologist, his research in recent years has led him into the fields of anthropology and linguistics in an attempt to understand better the influence of different cultural institutions, especially formal schooling, on the development of children. He is editor of *Soviet Psychology*, and his most recent book, co-authored with Sylvia Scribner, is entitled *Culture and Thought*.

BARBARA LLOYD is Reader in Social Psychology at the University of Sussex, author of *Perception and Cognition: a Cross-Cultural Perspective* and editor (with John Archer) of *Exploring Sex Differences*. Her interest in child development has always been strongly cross-cultural (her first research was published as part of the Whiting's *Six Cultures* study). She has recently investigated cognitive development among both English and Nigerian children.

THE DEVELOPING CHILD *edited by*

Jerome Bruner   Michael Cole   Barbara Lloyd

CHILDREN'S DRAWING

Jacqueline Goodnow

FONTANA/OPEN BOOKS

First published by Fontana/Open Books and
Open Books Publishing Limited 1977
Second Impression August 1980
© Jacqueline Goodnow 1977
Made and printed in Great Britain by
William Collins Sons & Co. Ltd, Glasgow
A hardback edition of *Children's Drawing* is available
from Open Books Publishing Limited
West Compton House, near Shepton Mallet, Somerset

Contents

Editors' Preface

Recent decades have witnessed unprecedented advances in research on human development. Each book in *The Developing Child* reflects the importance of this research as a resource for enhancing children's well-being. It is the purpose of the series to make this resource available to that increasingly large number of people who were responsible for raising a new generation. We hope that these books will provide rich and useful information for parents, educators, child-care professionals, students of developmental psychology, and all others concerned with childhood.

JEROME BRUNER *University of Oxford*
MICHAEL COLE *The Rockefeller University*
BARBARA LLOYD *University of Sussex*

Introduction
and Acknowledgements

Psychology can be pleasant. And it need not be complex or remote from everyday behaviour. Such apparently simple acts as scribbling, writing one's name, drawing a person or a road: all these are everyday activities but all raise interesting questions about the nature of children, the nature of skill, the nature of meaning.

My initial interest in drawings was largely sparked by the work of my own two children – Christopher and Mei-Mei. I have often saved old drawings rather than old photographs. Drawings provide a record of change and of times past made from the child's own point of view. They are also a source of constant wonder to children as they grow older, leading them to ask: 'Did I ever do things like that?' rather than the more usual question: 'Did I ever look like that?' To Christopher and Mei-Mei, who at seventeen and sixteen, gave permission for some of their early drawings to be used in this book, and to my husband Robert, who supported my long-term hoarding through many moves – my thanks.

Most of the material presented in this book stems from more recent years. It covers ideas I worked on in two places: George Washington University in Washington, DC, and Macquarie University, in Sydney, Australia. For direct assistance and the benefit of discussion, my thanks go to students and colleagues at both places: at George Washington, Marcia Bernbaum, Lila

Ghent Braine, Phyllis Evans, Nona Flynn, Sarah Friedman, Elyse Lehman, Rochelle Levine, and Richard Walk; at Macquarie, Roslyn Dawes, Diana Grafton, and Peter van Sommers.

For advice and cooperation, my debt is large to the New South Wales Department of Education and to the staff of many schools in both countries.

Together with the publishers, I should also like to thank Dr L. G. Braine and the Editor for permission to reproduce Figure (42) from the *Journal of Research and Development in Education*, Spring, 1973, 6, *No. 3*, 45; Professor F. E. Dart, Professor P. L. Pradhan and the Editor for permission to reproduce Figure (48) from 'The cross-cultural teaching of science', *Science*, 1967, *155*, 649-56 (copyright (1967) by the American Association for the Advancement of Science); and David Diringer and Hutchinson Ltd for permission to include Figure (41*b*) from *The Alphabet*, Vol. 2.

1 Why study children's drawings?

Why do children draw the way they do? The question has often been asked by parents and teachers, and also by the variety of scholars interested in the psychology of art, perception and thought. This small book is not intended as a review of all the research that has been done. Instead, it presents my own view, taking as a starting point recent research carried out by myself and a number of colleagues, and adding to it a selective account of earlier work and ideas. This research covers the usual children's pictures of humans, together with their copying of simple shapes (geometric or letter-like shapes) and their construction of maps: all referred to as 'drawing'. At first sight, such a wide usage of the term 'drawing' may seem strange, but it is common. We say, for instance, 'draw a person', 'draw this triangle', or 'draw me a map', using 'draw' wherever the essence of the task is work with lines and shapes on a flat surface.

In many respects, this book takes the form of a journey: a search for new ways of seeing, new ways of understanding, new ways of verifying and testing one's ideas. In this introductory chapter the first step is to ask: why be interested in children's drawings at all? The second is to consider some of the concepts and questions one might use in moving towards a clearer understanding of them. These concepts will underlie later chapters.

SOME REASONS FOR INTEREST

In part, our interest is a direct response to children's drawings in their own right. Most of them have charm, novelty, simplicity, playfulness, and a fresh approach that is a source of pure pleasure. They are simply 'good to look at', even if we have few words to describe why we find them so 'good'. But we are also interested because drawings are indications of more general phenomena of human life. They may be regarded as expressions of our search for order in a complex world, as examples of communication, as indices of the type of society we live in, as signs of intellectual development, as reminders of our own lost innocence and verve. Allied to these views of drawings as in a sense the tip of an iceberg is the thought that they are 'natural' rather than imitative – that they spring from within. If this is correct, then if we can understand them better we will have a better understanding of children and development in general. Small wonder that books on child development so often use children's drawings on their covers.

I, in fact, also subscribe to the view that children's drawings contain much beneath the surface, and in particular I shall argue that they are often indicative of general aspects of development and skill. Drawings can tell us something not only about children but also about the nature of thought and problem-solving among both children and adults.

To these constant bases of interest, we may add three more: first, the feeling that has grown up among psychologists that research should be more concerned with behaviour occurring in everyday environments, and less with complex special tasks in laboratory or clinical settings. What we learn from special tasks and special settings, it is now argued, can seldom be generalized to explain the everyday behaviour we initially wanted to understand. The problems in the way of generalization might be lessened if we worked directly with everyday behaviour, observing children in much the same way that ethologists observe birds or monkeys. Such pressures towards an ethological approach make simple graphic behaviour – copying, tracing, writing, mapping, making pictures – especially attractive for child-watchers.

A second reason is our increasing awareness that a great deal of thinking and communicating takes place visually. Over the last twenty years, analyses of communication have concentrated chiefly on words. In 1969, Rudolf Arnheim pointed out that our culture is preoccupied with words.[1]* He wanted to see 'words in their place', and more attention given to the visual aspects of thought and memory. Currently, some of his wishes are being met: for example, psychologists are increasingly attending to such topics as visual images in memory, body language in conveying a feeling or idea, the role of visual media such as television, and the impact on us of our visual environment.

The last reason, an important one, has to do with understanding the nature of action. Roughly speaking, a great deal of our interest in psychology and philosophy has been directed towards what Kevin Connolly and Jerome Bruner have called 'knowing that'.[2] We come to know that the number of objects in a set – peas on a plate, for example – remains the same whether they are pushed together or spread apart; we come to know that the week has seven days, that others may have a point of view different from our own, that dogs, cats and elephants all belong to the class called 'animals'. How this 'knowing that' develops is a topic of critical importance in psychology, especially when viewed in the light of those questions that have concerned Jean Piaget and his colleagues – questions such as: What lies beneath knowledge? How is it that

*Superior numerals indicate references on pp. 155-8.

information presented to us at one point is not absorbed or understood, whereas later we can take it in? What are the aspects of knowledge that mark a real step forward, that open up new doors rather than being just one more isolated piece of information?[3]

For all the importance of 'knowing that', it is not all there is to development. 'Knowing how' is equally important, though less often studied. We need to know, for example, how to search for an object or for information, how to get from X to Y, how to remember and how to learn, how to plan and organize a series of steps, how to keep track; in short, how to translate 'knowing that' into action. It is tempting to assume that once the information is in hand, then effective action will follow without problems. And psychology has been tempted. To take one example, we have been tempted to regard reversals and other orientation errors in writing and drawing as problems only in perception or in 'knowing that': the child is easily regarded as simply displaying 'perceptual problems' or as being indifferent to the importance of orientation. What the child sees or intends is clearly an important component, but it is not a sufficient explanation. In David Olson's words, no drawing is 'an automatic print-out of some perceptual world'. What is seen or intended must be translated into the action of drawing, and what we need to understand more fully is the nature of the translation and the nature of the action. This kind of point is not restricted to studies of drawing. It underlies, in fact, a wide-ranging trend to look more closely at the nature of 'knowing how', a trend that covers Bruner's and Connolly's studies of actions as apparently simple as a child reaching for an object, opening a box, or grasping a paint-brush;[4] John Flavell's analysis of 'serviceable' strategies for storing and retrieving what has been learned;[5] Bernstein's description of the nature of skilled physical movement,[6] and a host of questions about the nature of a 'plan' raised some time ago by George Miller, Eugene Galanter, and Karl Pribram, and still largely unanswered.[7]

These several interests – in the everyday world, the visual world, and the relationship between 'knowing that' and 'knowing how' – all help to focus attention on children's drawings. Not, of course, that drawings were not a focus of attention before. One wave of interest in the early 1930s, for instance, emphasized longitudinal studies and the possibility of describing change as a transition from drawing 'what one sees' to drawing 'what one knows should be there'. The approach reflected a search for ways of describing development and a belief – no longer widely held – that 'seeing' and 'knowing' are qualitatively different from one another. Another wave in the 1930s, reflecting a concern with education, stressed the analysis of pictorial skill and ways of developing it. A third, roughly in the 1950s and stemming from developmental psychology's increasing interest in tests and other predictive measures, stressed the use of drawings as indicators of intellectual level or emotional state. Given these previous waves, is there still much to be understood or said?

The answer to the first question is yes. For all the attention given to drawings, they are still mysterious. In addition, much of what we know is fragmented. Drawing pictures, copying geometric shapes, printing numbers or letters of the alphabet, copying or making maps are all called drawing and all have features in common, but they are typically assigned to separate areas; 'art', 'writing', and 'geography'. If we cannot find concepts that link them up, then we are a long way from understanding any of them.

In addition, much of what we know is at hunch level, with many ideas untested or tested only in a preliminary fashion. This question of 'testing' an idea is a complex one. Since my ideas about it underlie both my respect for much earlier work and the approach presented in this book, let me take a little time on it now. Basically, 'testing' involves two questions: What are we testing for? And how can we or should we test? Typically, we say that we test to see whether an idea is 'true' or not; and we judge truth by seeing how well an idea can bring out and pull together relationships between events, or how well it can predict some new event. In practice, however, we often judge an idea by its usefulness as well as its truth: even if wrong, or only partly true, we are interested in whether it gives rise to new questions, new ways of looking at phenomena so that now we see things in a different light or notice something we had not observed before. This 'utilitarian' view of ideas may cause some distress: it does not sit well, for example, with the concept of research workers only proposing or considering theories that are 'eternally true'. But *that* concept also causes distress, especially when we have to realize that most of our ideas are limited by what we currently know, influenced by when and where we live, and likely to be replaced by ideas seen as even more true than those we now hold.

In practice, also, we often do not check the usefulness or the truth of an idea by reviewing all possible cases, or by a full-scale experiment. It is often of value simply to point out a relationship – for example to point out that a drawing has certain features, or that two drawings are like one another in this way and unlike one another in that. The test of usefulness, in this respect, is whether the observer now has a new way of seeing or a new set of questions. Most analyses of art take this form. It is an extremely valuable form of testing, and it is not in fact limited to analyses of art (you can, for example, think of analyses of history in similar terms). But it is not the only check one can make. It is possible, for instance, to make a second check, in the form of seeing whether we are able to predict when certain kinds of drawing are likely to occur, or whether we can bring about certain kinds of drawings by setting up certain conditions. It is this second form of checking that we need to see more often in studies of children's graphic work.

The answer to the second question – are new concepts available? – is also yes. We will look at three general lines of psychology in the next section of this chapter. All of them are lines of work that hold promise as ways of overcoming the fragmentation of the area, making visible aspects we had not seen before, and leading towards experimental test. In addition, these three lines of work cut across a variety of interesting subjects – they are not unique to studies of graphics, so they hold out the promise of linking drawing to other behaviour: a two-way relationship that perhaps will add to our understanding both of drawing and of behaviour in general.

The three lines of work are (a) the analysis of patterns, (b) attention to sequence, and (c) study of questions of equivalence, or the nature of 'same' and 'different'. These three approaches underlie the material presented in subsequent chapters in this book. The analysis of patterns, for instance, is the focus of chapter 2; attention to sequence dominates chapters 3 and 4; and equivalence is the hub of chapters 5 and 6. In a sense, then, the next section is both an introduction to some general concepts and a preview.

Two themes run through all the chapters. One is a concern with the problem of description. In any kind of investigation, we need ways of pinning down the difference between one event and another, one production and another. Without ways of analysing similarity and difference, we cannot begin to ask questions about how what we observe (for instance features of drawings) relates to, for example, experience or age. I shall, in fact, take throughout the general position that the age of the artist is of less concern than our capacity to see what the similarities and differences are between drawings, regardless of a child's age.

The second theme is a concern with the consequences of

doing something in a particular way. We will be looking at the consequences of drawing in particular ways, but the question has general importance. When we notice something occur, it is always tempting to make our first question 'Why?'. I have tried to ask equally often the question 'So?'. Ways of working – ways of drawing – have consequences. With some methods, one step leads easily to a novel next step. With others, 'a problem solved is a problem created'. With more attention to consequences, we may increase the likelihood of understanding the nature of what we do, the nature of 'knowing how'.

WAYS OF APPROACHING DRAWINGS

ANALYSING SPATIAL PATTERNS

Any form of pattern presents a challenge, whether the pattern is an arrangement of cells, people's positions in a room, the placement of buildings in a city or features on a face, or the links between ideas or between people on a family tree. The challenge is first of all one of description. How can we describe a pattern? Especially, how can we describe it in terms that allow us to be specific about the differences between it and another pattern? And how can we use the description, particularly in ways that allow us to link the features of a pattern to some other event – link the pattern of streets, for instance, to ease of movement, the pattern of a face to an appealing effect, the pattern of ideas to ease in absorbing new information, or the pattern of cells to orderly growth or probable disaster?

This same challenge applies to drawings. They are patterns, made up of units or elements related to one another. The units may be of several kinds: dots, lines, circles, squares, blobs, masses, and so on. These are related in a variety of ways, with a variety of effects. The questions immediately arise: how are we to describe the units and their relationships? how do people come to select some units or relationships rather than others? and what are the consequences of such selection?

Under the term 'composition', questions of this sort have long been of interest to students of art. What arrangement of units produces effects of a particular type? What arrangements produce a sense of balance, unity, rhythm, movement, or surprise? A repeated unit or a symmetrical arrangement, for instance, helps create a sense of unity to a drawing; diagonal lines convey movement or tension; breaking a repeated pattern helps produce a sense of novelty.

Similar questions have also been of interest to observers of children's drawings. In chapter 2, we will look in some detail at contributions from three of these: Rudolf Arnheim,[8] Rhoda Kellogg,[9] and Drora Booth.[10] For the moment, let us take only one aspect of composition or arrangement, namely the

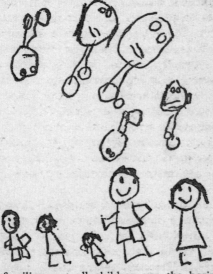

(1) Two families: not all children use the horizontal as a ground-line.

organization of a pattern around a reference point, especially around a 'ground-line' or 'stand-line'. Among adults, the horizontal is typically a base or 'ground'. Children, however, do not always observe this reference point. Some will draw all the members of a family standing on a common ground, but others will draw them in a way that leaves some, to our eyes, floating on air, or even upside-down (1). Equally common are chimneys drawn at 90 degrees to the roof-line rather than to the ground, or people drawn at 90 degrees to a line that stands for a hill.

The phenomenon – age differences in ground lines or reference points – is well established. The question – how do changes in reference points come about? – is another matter. Jean Piaget and Bärbel Inhelder argue that drawing chimneys at 90 degrees to a roof reflects a general aspect of intellectual development rather than simply an isolated feature of drawing.[11] They believe that children who do this are not yet able to use an overall point of reference for all the units in a drawing, but rely on one unit as a reference point for an adjacent one. When they arrange sticks in a series, for instance, or copy the layout of laundry on a line, they work from one item to the next rather than considering a set of items as a whole. Only when children can, among other things, cope with double or multiple relationships are they able to consider a more distant reference point: they must be able to think of the chimney as related to both the roof and the ground, just as one stick in the series is related to sticks on either side, or just as one person can be related in different ways to different people – be both someone's mother and someone else's sister or daughter. In turn, the ability to cope with multiple relationships depends upon the growth of what Piaget has termed 'operations', the capacity to carry out some change or transformation in one's mind rather than in physical reality – to imagine the effect of a transformation and to anticipate a result. In a sense, the eye can keep only one relationship in focus; the mind has to take care of the other.

What can we add here to knowledge about the way units are selected and put together? We shall certainly be concerned with reference points, but primarily in the context of the sequence of a drawing, with earlier steps in the sequence serving as reference points for later steps. Most of the research on patterns reported in chapter 2, however, takes a different tack. The emphasis there will be on differences between one pattern and another in terms of the number of units, the type of unit, and, in particular, the presence of boundaries or spaces between units. Let us anticipate for a minute, and consider the humans in (2). The first (2a) consists of units all carefully separated from each other: each hair, each tooth, each finger, each toe, exists in its own segregated space. In (2b), some units join: for instance the head and the torso touch one another, but with no shared boundary line. The third (2c) is a combination of joined and segregated units. And (2d)

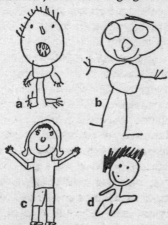

(2) Spaces as boundaries between units: parts of the body are completely segregated in (a), not at all in (d).

uses a single contour line to join together all parts of the body other than the head.

Boundaries, fences and spaces provide a way of describing differences among patterns. They are also an excellent focus for our interest in the consequences of using particular types of pattern.

To anticipate some of the material in chapter 2, one consequence of using different kinds of boundaries is the inclusion or omission of parts of the original. When children omit parts of a body – and they frequently leave out arms, hands and fingers – we often suspect that something odd is occurring in their perception of the world. All children should know that people have arms and so on, and that drawings should contain them. Why then do they so frequently leave them out?

One reason is the simple difficulty of including some parts within any particular form of construction. When the figure is based, for example, on an all-embracing line, as in (2d), it is difficult to include hands and fingers into flowing line. When children try, the results are often very strange (see chapter 2).

The nature of the line, then, may make some parts difficult to include. But equally often, omissions may stem from an interesting principle that underlies many children's patterns, a principle we may call 'to each its own space' or 'to each its own boundary'. Take, for example, the two humans in (3). The female on the left (3a) has curved arms – she has to because of her massive ear-rings. The female in (3b) has no arms: the space they would occupy is taken up by hair of Rapunzel length and thickness. We can see that it is not only that children often construct patterns in a way that leaves little or no space physically available on the page for certain parts: they also regard some space as not psychologically available. To use it would mean crossing boundaries, violating the space that belongs to another part or forms a comfortable 'no-man's land' between parts.

In brief, we can find ways of describing patterns that help describe differences among patterns and that have con-

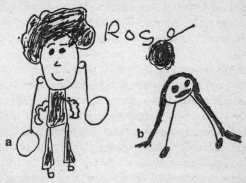

(3) The problem of available space: arms are omitted altogether, or else drawn to avoid crossing lines.

sequences. The same descriptions meet also a third criterion of usefulness: they overlap with forms of description used in subjects other than drawing. The idea of boundaries and their relative inviolability, for instance, has served well in describing relationships between ideas and between people – for people especially in terms of the physical spaces we try to maintain between ourselves and others. There is hope, then, of seeing in drawings some general aspects of behaviour that go beyond drawings.

LOOKING AT SEQUENCE

Sequence and direction are important aspects of many activities: driving a car, playing chess, walking, playing the piano, cleaning a house, asking questions, giving a talk, spending an allowance. In all these activities, the starting point often makes a difference to the success of the total action: 'Well-begun is half-done.' In all of them, also, each step affects later possible steps, either by increasing or limiting our options. Each purchase on a budget, for instance, affects what can be done with the money that remains. Each piece of furniture bought for a room makes a difference (or, to produce a particular effect, should make a difference) to later pieces. We may differ from one another in the constraints we allow the first step to place on later steps and in the way we cope with constraints, but earlier steps almost always have some effect.

This interest in sequence stems in part from the early work of K. S. Lashley, who argued the general point that understanding the nature of serial action was a key to understanding the nature of skill.[12] A broader base for our interest is the general rise of information theory – a theory from computer science that has produced some interesting insights into human behaviour. Information theory emphasizes chaining in behaviour and the description of changes in alternatives at each choice point in an action or decision, and can readily be applied to children's activities. To take one small example, psychologists have studied sequences in games of chance, in the way children play 'Twenty questions' or 'Animal, vegetable or mineral', and in the way we search for a name, a number, or a city on a page or map. The nature of a child's sequence is a guide to the development of his strategy or skill. It is also an example of a continuing problem in all forms of 'knowing how', namely the development of enough order in a sequence (enough to make it easy to keep track. for instance) without becoming so set in a routine that all flexibility is lost.

How do such points apply to drawings? By and large, sequences have been given little attention there. M. L. J. Abercrombie, David Olson and Alexander Marshack are exceptions. Abercrombie has been particularly interested in drawings by children with cerebral palsy and in how eye and hand movements are sequenced with one another.[13] Olson has put forward forcefully a general argument that children's graphic constructions should be viewed as a sequence of steps, each step calling for a choice between alternative next steps.[14] He has applied this argument to the way children copy lines on a checkerboard (horizontal, vertical, and diagonal) and to the problem of why diagonal lines are especially difficult to copy. The best known of the three, at least to people outside psychology, is probably Marshack.[15] His analyses of early cave-painting have challenged our image of early man as low in intellectual achievement, with few if any ways of analysing or recording complex events such as the passage of seasons, or the organization of time over a year. In Marshack's work, the analysis of meaning depends heavily on the analysis of sequence, as indicated by brush-work and other technical signs of order.

Can sequences help us understand children's work, both their drawings of humans and their construction of simple

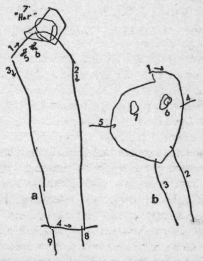

(4) How one child's sequence changed over two weeks.

geometric shapes and letters? A detailed answer to this question is the burden of chapters 3 and 4, but, to anticipate a little once again, sequence does in fact turn out to be a very useful tool. We can detect both differences in sequence among children, and also several consequences that follow from them.

In (4) for example, both drawings are by the same child. The earlier is (4a): its sequence starts in the centre, proceeds to the legs and returns for the topmost point, a 'hat'. Two weeks later, by (4b), the drawing has changed in proportions, and also in sequence. The start is at the top and the body parts are arranged in matched pairs (right leg, left leg; right arm, left arm; right eye, left eye).

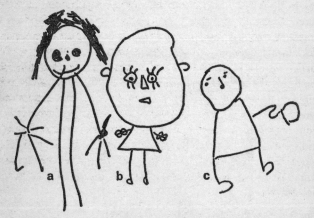

(5)   Sequence and possible omission: (a) and (b) used a top-to-bottom sequence and matched pairs, but sequence was not matched for (c) and the result is a missing arm.

Order can make a difference to whether anything is forgotten. For example, (5) shows three humans. The two on the left (a and b) are both drawn in a sequence of matched pairs (that is, one arm drawn immediately after the other, one leg drawn immediately after the other). Both also proceed from top to bottom with no return. Everything is orderly and nothing is forgotten (apart from what we would call the 'body' or 'torso' in the human on the left). In contrast, (5c) uses a scattered order and one arm has been forgotten. An orderly sequence, of course, is not the only way to make sure that all parts are included. Nor is it always helpful; an orderly sequence can be a hazard, increasing the likelihood of error when the usual sequence has to be modified or abandoned. This type of effect is particularly clear with errors in letter-like shapes (as we shall see in chapter 4).

In addition to the advantages and drawbacks of a routine, we shall see that sequence in drawings has another facet, which has to do with the way one part places constraints on later parts. Some of the most interesting aspects of children's drawings concern both the constraints they set for themselves (for example, the way they see later parts as 'in keeping with' earlier parts) and the way they often manage to escape some of the binds about to follow from an awkward first step. When we begin to see, as we shall in chapters 3 and 4, that sequential constraints help us make sense of many features of drawing – from omissions and upside-down humans to reversed letters, and even 'X-ray' figures (that is, figures with the body visible beneath the clothes) – then that apparently technical and mundane feature of drawings, sequence, comes into its more rightful place.

SEEING HOW EQUIVALENTS DEVELOP

A large part of our learning consists of coming to know that one thing may 'stand for' another or be called 'the same as' another: photographs reflect people, words stand for objects, the moon in all its phases is the same moon, certain animals belong to the same class – four-legged creatures in this group, for example, are called cats but in this group dogs. Some of this learning – same moon, same father with or without a beard, same mother with or without a hat – is called the recognition of identity. Part of it – the learning that words, photographs, and various squiggles on paper 'stand for' or 'correspond to' other objects or events – is called the learning of equivalents. The equivalents may even be related to each other: 'A' and 'a', for example, both 'stand for' the same set of sounds, and, in this respect, are 'the same as' one another.

Within this broad area of equivalence learning, we may talk about the perception of equivalents – essentially, the way we learn to read or decode an equivalent presented to us. We learn to know what certain words stand for; and we learn to read photographs, pictures and music.

We may also talk about the production or invention of equivalents, and this is the area of most interest for extension to children's drawings. How are equivalents developed? We may look at history as one source of information – the histories of language, or musical notation, or of art. In addition, we may look at children's inventions of equivalents, at the novel classifications they produce or at the new words they invent. A child who says, for instance, 'I am all muscled up with energy,' 'That tree has been timbered down,' or 'I want to be a type-writerer,' is inventing a new equivalent for a state of affairs that would conventionally be described in other terms. Inventions of this sort, we should note, are of major interest to students of language because they suggest that new equivalents are often developed by modifying something already in our repertoire, the modification being nicely in line with some specific rules. In effect, the underlying learning appears to be more a question of discovery and extension of rules than of imitation. If this is so, then it supports the view of children that has gained ground since the work of Piaget: that children participate positively in learning and actively construct their own views of the world.

How do such points apply to drawing? Drawings are

equivalents: they contain only some properties of the original, and convention frequently determines which properties should be included and in what way. To produce an 'acceptable' person or map, we usually require that some properties of the original be included (for instance, of appearance or position). Exactly which properties, however, may vary from occasion to occasion, from artist to artist, and from audience to audience. The dots or stick figures acceptable for a quick sketch are not acceptable as portraits. 'Realist' and 'abstract' artists, or children and adults, differ considerably in the number and types of features they include. And one audience may require a great deal of documentation before recognizing or accepting a drawing, while another audience may be, in E. H. Gombrich's terms, more ready 'to take a hint'.

As equivalents drawings are also ambiguous, and they vary in their relationships to what they stand for. Two or more equivalents may sometimes stand for the same thing: a dot, a line, a circle, a triangle, may all stand for a nose. And one equivalent may stand for two or more things: a circle may stand for a ball, a melon, a head, or a hole. This ambiguity is an important feature in not only children's drawings of humans, but also in the development of their maps, models, and diagrams.

Finally, drawing is an area where we have a chance to observe the way new equivalents are developed. E. H. Gombrich gives a number of delightful examples from the history of art that illustrate the way in which a new equivalent (such as the drawing of a new city or some exotic animal like a whale or rhinoceros) was often a minor modification of an old equivalent, even though meant to be 'true to life'.[16] Landscapes of 'new' countries by artists from 'old' countries are an especially good source for further illustrations. Early versions of the Australian landscape, for instance, are peculiarly English: the countryside is neat and green, the eucalyptus trees droop like willows, the rivers are gentle streams.

Given historical records, what can be gained by looking at children's inventions of equivalents in drawings? For one thing, history does not tell us a great deal about children: changes among adults from one era to another do not correspond at all exactly to changes among children as they develop. For another, children offer us the chance of exploring the invention of equivalents as we wish. We can ask for particular equivalents and observe directly how particular problems are solved.

To gain the most from these live records available to us, what should we ask for? In the work discussed in chapter (5), the focus is on equivalents likely to present difficulty, and so requiring either invention or a novel selection of properties to be included. To ask for 'a person', for example, is certainly to ask for an equivalent, but one that most children have practised to the point of routine formula. To ask for a map introduces something more novel; and it also forces a child to search for some way of indicating not simply the presence of objects but the relationships between them, namely their relative positions. To ask for an equivalent of something not itself visible (such as a sound) serves a similar purpose. So also does a request for something not usually included in drawings by children at a particular age (like movement in a person either running or bending over, at ages five to ten).

Looking at these specially requested drawings and at spontaneous drawings, we gain first of all a strong sense of respect for children's inventiveness. Take, for example, the spontaneous drawing shown in (6) made by a five-year-old boy whose sister had responded with more enthusiasm than expected to his ambiguous offer: 'You can have some of my french fries'. The spelling is itself an invention, an extension of some phonic rules, but the drawing is also an attempt at inventing a difficult equivalent – for movement. What this

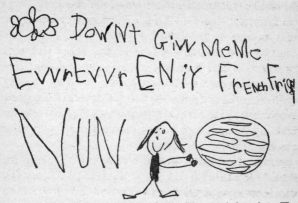

(6)   Inventing new equivalents in spelling and drawing. Translation: 'Don't give Mei-Mei ever ever any french fries, None.'

boy has done, moreover, is something we see over and over again in the development of new equivalents: he has modified the old version first of all by a change *in one part only*. In this case, only the arms are a departure from the usual figure.

We also frequently notice the difficulty of finding equivalents for relationships among objects or events. We can easily show two people or two buildings side by side: in effect, making a list of all the people or objects present in a scene. But to show them in contact or in a relationship with one another is a different matter.

Finally, we emerge from looking at equivalents with a healthy respect for the sheer quantity of learning required of children, both in becoming able to read the variety of visual equivalents a culture uses, and also in learning to produce the equivalents regarded as 'good' or 'acceptable'. Little of this learning seems to be directed explicitly by adults, but children apparently invest a remarkable degree of time and effort in observing the world around them and (to make a pun) in drawing conclusions.

Do these several points once again lead back to our understanding of the general nature of thinking and learning? The answer is yes. The results underline the importance of generally regarding children as actively engaged in learning, in abstracting and extending rules and principles. The results also raise a useful question for all areas involving change: where is the source of resistance? What parts of the old behaviour are the first and last to be modified? And – by no means least important – the results underline the extent to which development is a process of give and take, of two way interaction: the child's inventions on the one hand, the audience's response on the other, combined in a search for agreed-upon meanings.

2 Drawings as patterns

More clearly than most, children's pictures are made up of units combined in a variety of ways – some of this variety is illustrated in (7). The units may vary in type: for instance they may be straight lines, scribbled lines, circles, squares, triangles, or Latin crosses. Units may also vary in number: one or more ovals, for example, two or more stick-lines. And they may vary in the way they are joined to one another: stacked one above the other or linked by a common embracing contour.

How do children make their choice of units? What are the ways in which they combine them? And what are the consequences of choosing certain units or certain combinations?

SOME USEFUL CONCEPTS

The way units are put together is interesting from two quite separate standpoints, each with its own group of researchers. One group is concerned primarily with children's productions, and particularly with their progressions from one developmental stage to another. The other group is chiefly concerned with the general nature of art – with composition or the way some arrangements of units achieve better unity, balance, rhythm or surprise than others. D. A. Dondis is one of those interested in general aspects of composition;[1] Rhoda Kellogg and Drora Booth are two who concentrate on children's work, and Rudolf Arnheim spans both groups. For our current purposes we shall concentrate on Arnheim, Kellogg, and Booth and keep the focus on children's work.

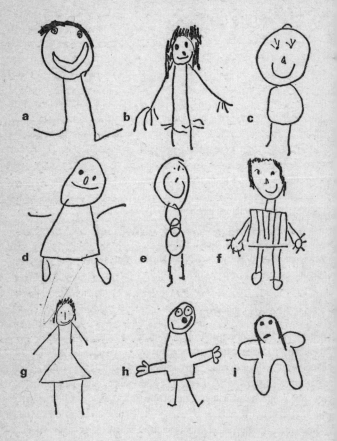

(7) The units children use to make humans vary greatly in type, in number, and also in how they connect up.

RUDOLF ARNHEIM

Arnheim is mainly concerned with how art relates to visual perception (that is, to what one actually sees) and to visual thought[2]. In brief, he proposes that what we draw is not a replica but an equivalent of the original. That means that what we draw contains only some of the properties of the original – though it must of course resemble it to an extent. Arnheim believes that the units we choose to make our equivalents are based on the 'structure' of the original; they are the aspects that are the essence of its form and that underlie our recognition of it. The basic 'structure' of the human figure, for example, is given by its vertical axis, and so it is this verticality that children incorporate in their drawings. In contrast, the horizontal aspects are less essential and may easily be neglected.

Our equivalents, according to Arnheim, are developed within the limits of the medium: that is, first of all, within the limits of the *graphic* medium. Finger-paints, sponges, pencils, thick and thin brushes, all give rise to different effects. They also make us more or less likely to produce different units. With a pencil, for instance, lines come readily to hand. With thick paint and a large brush, blobs or masses are more likely. But 'medium' can also have a second, more subtle, meaning: not the tool, but the set of concepts one has available, the visual vocabulary at one's disposal. As an analogy, consider what happens when one first uses a foreign language. Conversations have to be steered into areas one can discuss. Questions have to be phrased so that answers can be understood. Many a novice who starts off, for example, with 'Where is the railroad station?' soon learns to ask: 'Is the railroad station in this direction?' which yields, hopefully, a yes or no answer. One also comes to use a few simple phrases over and over again, stretching them – with small changes in tone or an occasional extra word – to meet a variety of occasions.

Both the search for structure and the limits of graphic vocabulary may underlie a single aspect of children's drawings. Take, for instance, the way children often make repeated use of the same graphic unit, especially for arms and legs. In (8*a* and *b*) the units used for arms and legs are alike both in shape and in orientation. In the remaining examples, legs and arms differ in orientation, but retain their similarity in shape and size. The drawing (8*h*) illustrates a different but common form

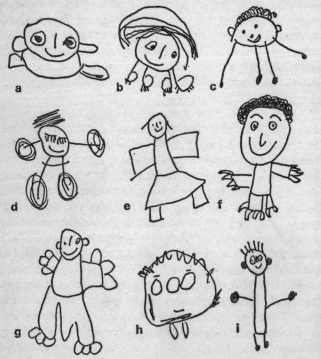

(8) Economy: the same unit used for both arms and legs, for eyes and nose, or for ears, hands and feet.

of economy: the same unit, repeated in a straight line with no variation in size, serves for the nose and both eyes.

An economical use of shapes produces a sense of unity in a child's drawing. In addition, economy represents an achievement of visual thought, the discovery that the same unit can be used for more than one purpose. Arnheim himself mentions a particularly striking example: a drawing where a heart shape is used in varying sizes and proportions for eyes, ears, mouth, brooch, arms – in short, wherever feasible. In his view 'the device' (that is, the heart shape) 'displays all the traits and functions of a concept. It serves to make understandable a number of different objects which resemble it sufficiently to be subsumed under it . . . It establishes a bit of order in a world of complexity.'[3] In effect, what may appear at first sight to be a limited vocabulary of units may represent a conceptual strength, a discovery of similarity.

RHODA KELLOGG

For Arnheim, units and arrangements are chiefly determined by the need for structure, the search for order, and the presence of visual concepts. For Kellogg, a search for order and balance is also critical.[4] She too believes that units and arrangements at any one stage in development reflect what has been happening at earlier stages. She sees scribbles as the first stage. These scribbles are explored in various 'placements' on a surface and later developed into simple shapes or basic 'diagrams' such as circles or rectangles. Children then link pairs of diagrams into 'combines' (for example two circles attached to one another), or combine three or more into 'aggregates' (perhaps a circle, with spokes made from two intersecting crosses). Among these several combinations, they are inclined to prefer and repeat just a few. It is these preferred combinations that they adapt to represent objects and people.

Kellogg thinks that at every stage children respond continually to the presence of order in a shape. They try out numerous scribbles, diagrams and combinations, but the units they remember and repeat are those that have good visual form, or good balance. The mandala – a closed form, usually ovoid, with crossed lines – is one of her favourite examples (9*d*). In Kellogg's terms, this is a form that displays excellent balance, a combination of unity and contrast. It is this balance, she proposes, that accounts both for the appearance of the mandala in many historical forms of art, and also for children's delight with it at every age. 'Suns' or 'radials' are a similar kind of form and are repeated in the same way (see 9*a*, *b* and *c*).

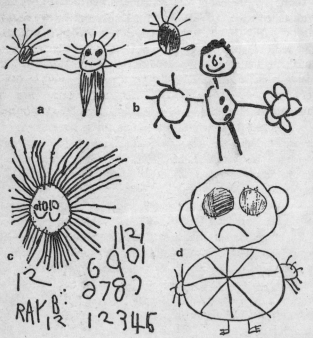

(9) Patterns incorporating favourite units (such as radials or mandalas) into human figures.

The 'sun' combines both contrast in the type of line and balance in the way one of the units (the line) is repeated and rotated in regular fashion around the constant focus of the other (the circle). Kellogg believes that these forms of visual order are *intrinsically* attractive – we do not have to learn they are 'good' shapes. The reason for that may lie in some properties of the visual system, or it could be that they match with a simple human liking for order in all aspects of life: 'a primary visual order exists in every mind.'[5]

The search for order and balance is Kellogg's first factor. The second factor she sees underlying units and arrangements is the way drawings at any one stage incorporate units that mark an earlier stage. This incorporation may take two forms. Most directly, the earlier units can simply become part of the later work. The radials that originally stood by themselves as 'suns' or 'flowers' may come to be used for hands (8*b*); a mandala shape may become part of a human torso (8*d*). Very frequently scribble lines get incorporated into a human shape (10). They may be used, with either exuberance

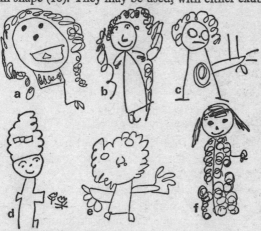

(10)   Scribble: restraint or exuberance.

or restraint, for hair (*a*, *b* and *c*). Or the same looping lines may also serve to form a hat, a single outline for head-and-hair combined, or the mass of the body itself (*d*, *e* and *f*).

Less directly, an earlier stage may influence the overall arrangement of units. Kellogg finds this especially true for humans: in a sense, her humans betray their origins. Here are some examples:

Humans drawn with their hair on end or with limbs like the spokes of a wheel may reflect their evolution from an earlier 'radial' or 'sun' shape (11 *a*, *b* and *c*).

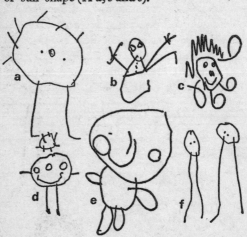

(11)   Parts or even whole figures may reflect their derivation from a favourite radial, mandala or oval.

Humans with arms that fall on the same axis, either horizontal or diagonal, may reflect their evolution from an earlier mandala shape (11 *d* and *e*).

Humans with no arms at all may reflect a preference for an overall shape, such as an oval. 'All children make the armless human, and they do so *after* they make the human with arms. The reason for omitting arms is not immaturity or forgetfulness; it is simply that such a human looks better to the child ... once he has made the head and the legs in certain proportions' (f).[6]

Rhoda Kellogg's hypotheses are enormously provocative and well worth further study. We need, however, to note that there are two possibilities. Certainly a later form may resemble a first because it has been derived from it, but the two may equally well be similar because they both observe the same

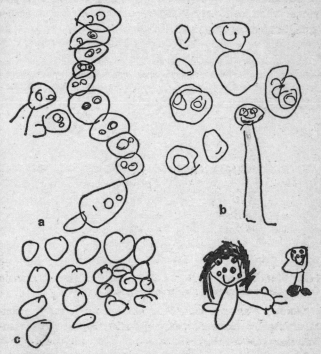

(12) Designs developing into pictures: (a) and (b) were produced by two children in a single session; the most human figures were drawn last. In (c) circles drawn at one session are included as facial features in the next.

principles – the principles that determine what is pleasing in one kind of drawing may apply just as much to the other, regardless of which comes first. To sort things out, we need to supplement Kellogg's analysis by looking at progressions within the work of individual children. Some examples are shown in (12): in (a) and (b), a child's exploration of concentric circles becomes a direct part of a human figure, drawn on the same page but towards the end of the work. In (c), the circles explored for all of one drawing session appear as features of a face on a later day. A great deal more evidence of this type is needed to test Kellogg's arguments. Her work, however, does greatly strengthen our sense of component units in drawing, and it also underlines the importance of asking how children come to select particular units and particular arrangements of units.

DRORA BOOTH

Both Rhoda Kellogg and Drora Booth worked in centres for young children, were impressed by children's work, and were led to wonder, observe, and collect over considerable periods of time: Rhoda Kellogg in San Francisco, Drora Booth in Argentina and Australia. Like Kellogg, Booth also believes that a search for order is a fundamental characteristic of humans, that 'the arts interpret the human mind', but her interest in order is directed primarily towards patterns – to work where the primary intention is a design rather than a 'picture' that stands for and visibly resembles an object or person.[7]

Within designs, Booth has been interested in how children use two main units: lines and dots. The novelty of her approach lies in looking at arrangements in terms of the 'transformations' children bring to bear on these units: transformations such as repetition, or rotation around a central point as in a star-shape or a sunburst.

Booth's most specific observations are based on children aged four and five years in an Australian pre-school – children using paint and brushes and encouraged to produce anything they liked, without pressure towards drawing objects or people. Most of them were observed over a school year, and the patterns they produced were divided into three categories: scribble, topology (colours separated in masses or spots without clearly defined order), and pattern (clear signs of order). Over the year, she noted three points: first, that the most common progression was from scribble to topology to pattern but there were frequent shifts back and forth as children explored different ideas, colours, and techniques. Secondly, that of the two elements of pattern (lines and dots), lines were usually discovered first. And third, that the first form of order to be used was repetition, typically repetition of a line (as in 13a). Later forms consisted of rotation around a point (13b) and reflection (13c, d and e), with reflection around a horizontal or vertical line appearing before reflection around a diagonal.

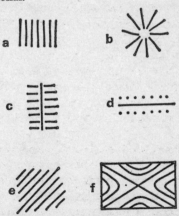

(13) For most children, repetition (in increasingly complex forms) is the earliest manifestation of order.

Booth's approach is valuable in two respects. First, it offers a way of linking children's work to a general theory of intellectual development, that of Jean Piaget and his colleagues. One of the basic tenets of this theory is that a great deal of knowledge consists of learning about transformations and their effects; we learn that quantity (a pound of sugar, for instance) remains the same even though the shape of the container changes; that number remains the same whether items are spread out or piled in a heap; or that distance up a hill is the same as distance down – for all the difference in effort. Similar discoveries, Booth suggests, underlie the child's increasing understanding and use of various transformations in art work. The capacity to discover and use transformations in both art and science might in fact depend on a common underlying intellectual growth.

The second value of Booth's approach is less theoretical: it draws our attention to the importance of patterns or designs in their own right. Part of our cultural heritage is a stress on realism, with the result that we often convey to children two messages: patterns and pictures should be kept separate from

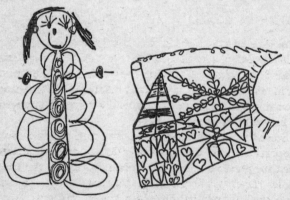

(14) Two 'decorative' drawings, combining 'design' and 'pictorial' units.

one another, and pictures are better. The first message leads to a decline in pictures that are attractive because of their 'decorative' units and arrangements (14), and often to a declining interest in producing art. According to T. Munro 'with advancing age, the sensuous delight in colour, form, and line for their own sake is sacrificed to the dominating interest in representing certain types of subject matter and in doing so with utmost realistic accuracy.'[8] The second message – pictures are better – often leads to teachers and adults discouraging the exploration of designs or 'decorative art'. It is only in relatively recent times that we have been exposed to adult art that has little concern for realism, that appears to consist mainly of patterns but is still accepted as respectable 'art'. As a result, the invention of patterns is currently an accepted and valued part of a school's art curriculum, at least for young children (though there is still some generation lag to be overcome). Many an adult, for example, has recently been cautioned not to ask 'What is it?'. And many a parent has been puzzled by a pre-schooler's apparently sophisticated answer: 'It's a design'.

THE ORGANIZATION OF UNITS

Arnheim, Kellogg, and Booth all help to make explicit two valuable sets of questions: first, how are we most usefully to describe the organization of units in a drawing? Suggested so far in this chapter have been descriptions in terms of repetition, economy, symmetry, rotation around a point, or arrangement to fit within certain proportions.

Secondly, what principles can we single out that underlie the organization or arrangement of units? Several have already been suggested: a search for order and balance, the effect of earlier stages, a preference for particular shapes and transformations, the relative difficulty of transformations.

But are there additional ways of describing and accounting

for the organization of units in a drawing? In particular, are there ways that can be easily specified and that lead on to experimental checks of a plausible idea?

Suppose we return to a question mentioned in the introduction – namely, the ways children use boundaries and separations between parts as a way of describing organizational patterns. In (7f) for instance, boundary lines mark each body-part off from the others: each limb, each part of the torso has its own fence. At the other extreme, (7i) uses an all-embracing line, a single boundary that combines the entire body into a single unit.

Alternatively, the separation and combination of areas may depend on the way children use overlapping space. The wheels of trains, for example, sometimes overlap, for instance in (23b). More often, however, young children avoid overlapping space, and seem to prefer a sort of no-man's land between parts. All told, young children seem to operate with two general principles: to each its own boundary, and to each its own space.

Can we make effective use of separations and boundaries as ways of describing the patterning of units in children's drawings? The next two sections are concerned with this question. The first of the two is based on 'free' drawings – that is, drawings produced without adult request or at a simple request just to 'draw a person'. The second is based on 'constrained' drawings – drawings where we have deliberately faced the children with a problem of boundaries, asking them to complete a figure that invites the crossing of lines.

LINES AND BOUNDARIES: FREE DRAWINGS

A variety of embracing lines is shown in (15). They range from cases where the contour combines head and neck to cases where it embraces the whole body. These embracing contours combine two or more areas into one. They are different from shared boundaries, where two areas (such as head and torso) may have some fence in common but remain separate.

Why regard embracing contours as a significant aspect of pattern? For three reasons. First, embracing lines make a difference to what can be done: they open up the possibility of different qualities to a figure – static figures can become more fluid, more playful, more expressive of movement. Secondly, a

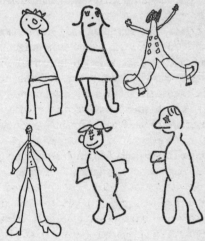

(15) Single contours extended to embrace a variety of body parts.

shift from separate units to embracing lines must be a major one intellectually as well as artistically. The child must mentally have constructed not simply a list of parts but a number of interacting relationships between parts. Thirdly, we have some grounds for expecting the ability to use embracing lines to be related to age. In copying simple shapes, such as squares, children move from their early use of separate lines to the use of continuous or all-embracing lines; in the USA, and probably in similar cultures elsewhere, children use continuous lines maximally at about the age of seven. And a simple inspection of drawings of humans will easily confirm that they also show embracing lines occurring at a later age than a complete separation of units.

A close relationship between embracing lines and chronological age, however, does not appear to be the most promising link to look for at this point. We know, from work on simple shapes, that the relationship to age will not be a straightforward one: with simple shapes, 'threading' (laying out a contour as if it were a continuous thread) shows a rise and then a fall, at least in the USA. The same might well be true for the more complex drawings of human figures. We also know that children at one and the same age often draw humans in a variety of ways: the same child may use a whole range of techniques within a single day, week, or month. For this reason, incidentally, Rhoda Kellogg points out how dangerous it is to use children's drawings – particularly a single drawing – as a measure of intelligence.[9] Finally, we might well suspect that units and arrangements will vary with the artists' purpose.

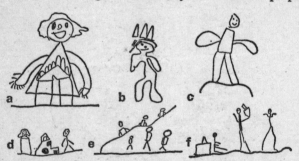

(16)   Figures drawn by a five-year-old boy over two months: the star humans in the top row get a far more complex treatment than the extras in the action scenes below.

Drawings collected over two months from one five-year-old
re shown in (16). This boy drew relatively complex people
when these stood alone or were the stars in the scene (*a, b, c*:
my sister'; 'me at a birthday party'; 'I am standing on a rock').
He drew much simpler figures when they were part of a scene
where the action and its setting were the major features
d, e, f: 'we walked in the city'; 'we climbed a hill'; 'we danced
in the sand').

The more profitable link appears to be one that relates to the
use of embracing lines to end-results in drawings, especially
those end-results that appear to us to be 'errors', or to be major
areas of difference between drawings by adults and by children.
One such relationship appears in (17). When a single

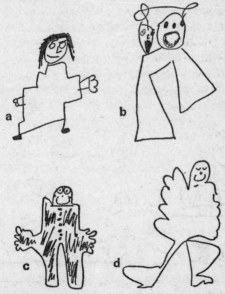

(17) An all-embracing line, especially combined with a full
quota of fingers, can produce some splendidly bizarre results.

embracing line is used for a human, the figure becomes more
playful. The line is also more difficult to control and the end
result may be a figure we regard as bizarrely out of proportion.
The effects are particularly striking when children operate
with two principles, both of which are important to them, for
example when they use an embracing line *and* incorporate
within this line a carefully counted-out set of five fingers like
(17c and d). The end-result may look more like a big bird than
a human, which could be a source of delight to children but
also a source of probable misinterpretation by adults.

A second consequence exemplifies the saying: 'a problem
solved is a problem created'. When embracing lines are used
the hand is often omitted or is at best a mitten-shape (18a,
and c). This effect can occur equally when the embracing line
covers the whole body, or when it covers only a part of it. In
fact, both hand and arm may be omitted altogether.

How else do children solve the new problem of embracing
lines *plus* hands? One way is to add hands on to the initial core.
The flowing line then often produces hands like bunches of
bananas or boxer's gloves (18d, e and f). Alternatively, they
may try to incorporate the hand within the line used for the
solid arm. The further problem now is to combine the width
required for several fingers with the width required for an arm.
The end-result may be an arm that is massive throughout, like
a tree-trunk, or that fans out from a thin wrist like a paddle
(18 g–k).

These consequences are especially worth understanding. It
is tempting, for example, to infer from bird-winged humans
that the child is misperceiving, or to infer from over-sized
hands that these have a special emotional significance. A
simpler and likelier explanation, however, would seem to be
the difficulty of anticipating the problems that each new use of
line turns out to create.

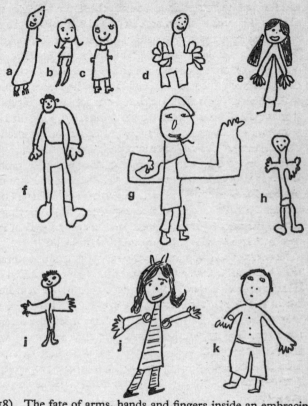

(18)   The fate of arms, hands and fingers inside an embracing line.

TO EACH ITS OWN SPACE

So far we have found separations and boundaries useful as ways of describing change and pointing out consequences. But we have not yet achieved our additional goal of using these concepts in a properly experimental manner. If a way of describing drawings is to be fully checked, then we should be able to set up an experimental situation where we can demonstrate that the particular principle involved is indeed important to children. The demonstration should not be *post hoc*; that is, we should be able to say before the drawings are made that they will be of a particular type.

In two studies, we have been concerned with this experimental criterion. Both start from the hypothesis that young children will avoid overlapping spaces. Both involve presenting children with a situation where overlapping spaces provide one solution to a problem, and both predict that a variety of solutions will be attempted in preference to overlapping.

FIRST STUDY: HUMANS WITH ARMS AND HAIR

In drawing humans, children frequently find that the arms, hair and ears they wish to draw all frequently compete for the same space – they all may be drawn out from the single circle. If lines are not to cross and spaces not to overlap, how is the problem to be solved?

One solution is to omit a part. As Rhoda Kellogg points out, 'children seldom draw both arms and hair on a head.'[10] Which part is omitted may vary from child to child or from occasion to occasion. In one classic case of omission and misinterpretation, for example, I interpreted lines drawn from a single circle as 'hair' and was told: 'No, arms'. A week later, my confident interpretation of the same lines was again corrected: 'No, hair.' On two subsequent occasions, 'hair' and 'arms' again appeared in alternate fashion, each departing from the scene when the other appeared.

If we block omission as a solution, what will children do? Will they abandon the principle of not crossing lines, or will they find some other solution? Suppose, for instance, that we offer young children a partly drawn human consisting of one circle and two vertical stick-lines, and ask them to add both arms and hair. The children might still squeeze in both, perhaps abandoning proportion rather than cross lines or shift from the usual pattern of attaching both arms and hair to the single solid. Alternatively, they might be prompted to relocate the arms so that they emerge from the stick-lines rather than from the circle. In these cases, we should say that the principle of not crossing lines was more important to them than the usual patterning. We might also begin to suspect that new patterns might, in spontaneous drawings, emerge from a wish both to include more parts and, at the same time, to maintain the principle of not crossing lines.

In all, we used three ways of precipitating such problems: (a) by asking for both arms and hair on a circle-and-sticks figure; (b) by asking for hair on a figure where the arms were in the way; and (c) by asking for arms where the hair was in the way. The original drawings, and several types of solution, are shown in (19, 20, 21, and 22).

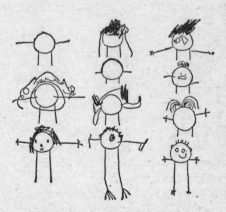

(19) How do children add hair and then arms (or arms and then hair) to a given figure (single circle, vertical stick lines)? The solutions in the left-hand column, where the hair crosses the arm-lines, are much rarer than the others.

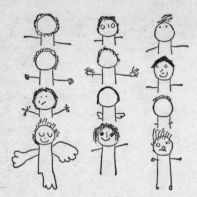

(20) A second type of solution: these children have drawn arms from the vertical sticks rather than from the circle, which they would usually do when drawing freely. In the first column, the hair covers all or most of the space now available, while in the third it is kept well separated from the arms.

When both arms and hair are to be added, the first choice is between placing both as lines drawn out from a single circle or placing one set of lines further down the 'body'. Of the sixty pre-schoolers, one-third chose to place the arms out from the 'legs' – far more than we would expect in spontaneous drawings of similar circle-and-stick type. (The same classes in the same school, a year earlier, drew 'arms' out from 'legs' in only one-tenth of the circle-and-stick humans they produced). So we can apparently shift the location of one part by putting two parts into competition for the same space. Among those who did not adopt this solution but drew both parts out from the circle, only three children crossed the lines of arms and hair. The others adopted a variety of arm-positions and hair-styles that avoided crossing barriers.

When hair is to be added to a figure with arms already extending from the single circle, it isn't feasible to solve the problem by relocating the arms. But even then, few children

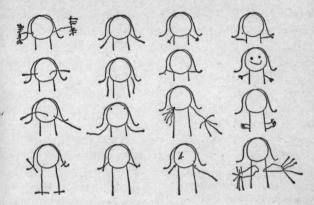

21) Adding arms to a figure that already has hair: the arms can cross the hair, but that is unusual. Otherwise they point downwards at a steep angle or emerge at their usual 90 degrees from the vertical 'legs'.

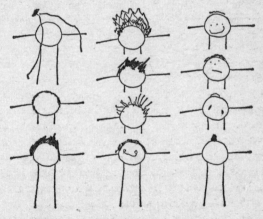

22) Adding hair to a figure that already has arms: the last two figures in the right-hand column are wearing hats instead, because there was 'no room' for hair on this figure.

cross the arm and hair-lines, although many allow the two
parts to touch. Particularly interesting are those children who
declare the problem impossible but offer to add a hat rather
than hair (right hand column of 22). It is always a source of
wonder that children draw hair standing up like wire, or draw
so many humans with hats in an era when few people wear hats.
The mystery disappears, however, if we think of hats and wiry
hair as features that can be drawn on to the single circle
without competing for space required for other features.

Finally, consider the children asked to add arms to a human
with flowing hair. Again only a few children cross hair and
arms. Most solve the problem by changing the usual angle of
arm-lines or by moving the arm-lines farther down the figure
than is customary.

We can, then, set up experimental situations where we can
test the strength of commitment that children have to the
boundary principles suggested by their free drawings. In turn
we begin to find some ways of understanding aspects of free
drawings that might otherwise seem mysterious or be attributed
to some oddity in children's perception of the world.

SECOND STUDY: THE WHEELS OF A TRAIN

Children often produce drawings apparently according to
'aerial perspective' – that is, drawn as they might possibly look
from the air, or if squashed. The first train in (23) is an example
– two wheels 'above' the carriage, two wheels 'below' it.

Animals or insects may appear the same way. How do such
drawings come about? Partly as a result of a lack of any strong
attachment to the idea that only the bottom of the page stands
for the ground. But partly also because space where legs or
wheels would normally be drawn has already been taken up.
On one occasion N. H. Freeman tried an experiment with a
child who had just drawn an animal figure with two legs above

and two below. He presented the child with a partially-drawn horse where the rider already occupied the space above the body. This time, the child placed all four legs in the usual lower space.[11]

Roslyn Dawes and I tried a similar experiment, pre-empting the lower rather than the upper space. We gave children a drawing of a train: a single carriage with two large wheels. We then said: 'the child who drew this wanted to put in two more wheels, but didn't know how to do it. Could you finish the drawing?'

This request actually faced the children with a number of problems. Ideally, the new wheels ought to be of the same size and shape as the two already drawn. They would be attached to the underside of the carriage and not extend beyond it. And they would touch the same ground. To achieve all this, the wheels would have to be drawn to overlap either as two complete circles or with one circle incomplete. Since we know that overlapping solutions are rare in spontaneous drawings, we can predict that other solutions will be found. One of them is likely to be placing the two extra wheels in the space more freely available.

The variety of ways children adopted to solve the problem is shown in (23): 'aerial perspective', as in (23a); over-lapping wheels – seen only once in a group of close to 100 children aged three to seven (b); the use of space at the side (c); changes in the size and shape of the new wheels (d, e and f); and finally, a triumphant creation of appropriate new space by adding extra parts to the train (g and h).

To avoid overlapping, children are clearly ready to give up some other requirements they normally meet, like drawing wheels of the same shape or size. The effect is what we would expect in problem-solving: that is, to meet one goal we will often sacrifice another. Especially characteristic of problem-solving are the delightful solutions in (g and h), where the

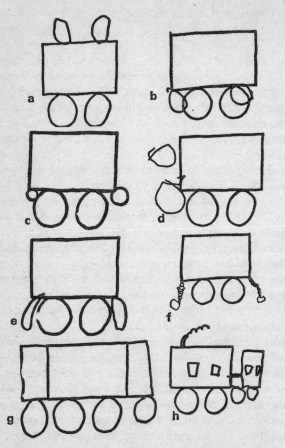

(23) How do you add two more wheels to a train, where two
wheels have pre-empted much of the lower space?

problem has been overcome by redefining the initial constraints
the initial terms or premises that created the bind. In effect
the problem has been redefined and the difficulty wiped out

PATTERNS AND SEQUENCES

Up to this point, we have considered the relationships of parts of drawings to one another and to the page. The concepts we have drawn upon may be applied to any completed drawing: concepts such as economy of units, number of parts, type of line, arrangements to allow each part its own boundary and its own space. We have proposed that many features of children's drawings may be attributed to the way they solve problems encountered in the course of achieving certain kinds of patterns or problems created by their own achievements.

At this point, let us step aside briefly from drawings. We are about to look at a somewhat different aspect of drawing – namely, sequence. Before doing so, however, think about the notion of pattern in a wider context. Patterns are all around us. They may be physical: look, for example, at the way people form clusters and spaces when sitting in a bus, restaurant, or library. They may also be conceptual: our ideas form clusters, are sorted into different compartments, are close to or remote from one another. Graphic, physical, conceptual: is it possible that all patterns have similar features or can be described in similar terms? Finding such similarities is a source of pleasure and reassurance: they provide both a sense of 'elegant economy and a sort of reassurance that one is 'on the right track', not inventing a complete new set of terms that have no relevance outside a small world. For such reasons, mathematicians often find delightful the analysis of graphic patterns: they can, for example, see both mathematics and graphic designs as based on a limited set of transformations. For those interested in such approaches, H. S. M. Coxeter's analysis of the work of Escher is an example.[12]

Less esoterically, you may wish to note that one of the concepts used to analyse children's graphic patterns in this chapter is similar to one used in the analysis of physical and conceptual patterns. This is the notion of describing patterns in terms of the use and nature of boundaries or spaces. In analysing physical patterns, psychologists such as Michael Argyle use the distances we keep from one another as one way of describing the organization of territory and our sense of comfortable space. The comfortable distance may vary from one individual to another and from one culture to another, but all of us share a sense of 'own space' and all of us share a sense of unease when the distance we regard as appropriate is ignored and a boundary is 'violated'.

Conceptual patterns may be thought of in similar terms. The best example of such an approach is the work of Kurt Lewin, who, back in 1935, proposed that we think of ideas and 'life-spaces' as regions, varying in size and proximity to one another as well as in terms of the permeability or rigidity of a boundary.[13] Where boundaries are not permeable, ideas or parts of ideas or parts of one's life simply exist side by side, touching but forming separate compartments. Change in thought or in life-style was, for Lewin, similar to the changes we observe in drawings, that is, often a matter of change in the number, the location, and the firmness of boundaries.

To lower our sights once more to drawings: some of the effects suggested in this chapter are not only matters of pattern. They are also affected by sequence. It is often the early parts of a drawing, for example, that set the problems of how to add a further part without crossing lines or violating the space that belongs to another unit.

How much can we learn from a more direct study of sequence? Will children's sequences in drawing display a different facet of the development of order or stability in their behaviour? Will they provide a key to some other constraints or principles that children regard as important in constructing a drawing? These questions take us to the next chapter.

3 Sequence in children's drawings

Does the sequence of drawing in children's pictures help account for the pictures drawn? If so, what is it about a given sequence that leads to a particular effect?

In searching for an answer we can draw data either from free or from constrained drawings. Free drawings, of course, are those children produce however they please, either for their own enjoyment or at our request. With constrained drawings, though, we start with one section already drawn and ask for the drawing to be added to or completed. As a rule, constrained drawings are used to provide a way of checking experimentally ideas derived from free drawings.

Perhaps most notable about sequences in drawings is the degree of order and consistency children reveal, even as young as three, four, or five. At a time when in much of their behaviour they appear whimsical, irrational, or easily distracted by the last thing to come along, their drawings reveal a great deal of order. In a sense, they proceed according to plan. To me, the discovery of this orderly sequence is as important and exciting as the finding that young children's language follows discernible rules, or as Lila Ghent's finding that young children are very consistent in their judgements about whether abstract shapes (or their own designs) are 'upside-down' or 'right-side-up'.[1] In all three cases children's behaviour follows an identifiable principle that can be seen to change with age.

So the apparent disorder in children's behaviour – its apparent lack of principles or rules – is due to our own ignorance of the principles they work by.

Sequences also draw our attention to the problem-solving element in children's drawings. Problems tend to arise as a consequence of following particular sequences and the solutions to these problems help account for the nature of the final drawings.

There is, for example, a relationship between sequence and the inclusion or omission of parts. The easiest way for a part to be included is for it to be embedded in an orderly sequence. Once outside the safe circle of a routine order, parts of a human may easily be forgotten. Their inclusion is subject to the vagaries of a final inspecting eye, an eye that may or may not be alert for missing items.

It is also true that early steps in a sequence may place constraints or limits on later steps. One of these was mentioned in Chapter 2; it was the constraint of not crossing lines, of respecting the space or the boundary allotted to other parts of a figure: a constraint essentially of 'psychologically available space'. In this chapter, we shall be concerned, to begin with, with the constraints of physically available space and, at greater length, with those of agreement or 'reasonable fit' between earlier and later units in a drawing: agreements in the type and the orientation of the units. As with children's problem-solving in other fields, the fascinating aspects revolve around the way constraints of various kinds are accepted, evaded, or creatively negated.

FREE DRAWINGS

How are we most usefully to describe sequences? We can note whether children work from top to bottom. Or whether they use a pair as a single unit, for instance both eyes, both arms, both legs, drawn as a pair that is completed before moving on. Thirdly, we can note left-right order, especially within a pair: left and then right eye, and so on. In this section, we shall work backwards: starting with left-right sequences, and then moving on to pairing and the use of a top-to-bottom order.

LEFT-RIGHT SEQUENCES

Among school children, we often observe a left-right sequence for arms and legs. Is the order used by pre-schoolers as well? Suppose we start with drawings where the sequence is easy to count and where the drawings all have the same three units: humans that consist only of a single circle and two stick 'legs'. We can then move to a set with two additional units: all the humans consist of a single circle and four stick-lines, two 'legs' and two 'arms'. The first set contains 39 drawings, the second 40. The 79 are all examples of their kind found among 273 Sydney pre-schoolers (aged three to five) who produced a recognizable human when asked to 'draw a person'. The broad range of the drawings and the variety of arm positions are revealed in (24).

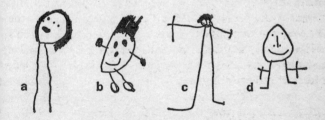

(24) Four types of stick-and-circle drawings, varying in the number and position of sticks. In a collection of 79 drawings these types (a), (b), (c) and (d) occurred 39, 33, 3 and 4 times respectively.

Pre-schoolers in fact show a clear preference for right-left order. Among the 39 armless humans, 29 of the legs were drawn in right-left order, 10 in left-right. Among the 40 humans with arms, 25 were right-left and 14 left-right. The remaining child used a broken order: right leg, arms right-left, and then left leg.

A left-right order appears then to be a later development and it is probably the effect of learning to write English script. The same also probably applies to drawing circles: older children rather consistently use a counter-clockwise direction for a single circle, but 40 of our 79 pre-schoolers used clockwise. If these Sydney children grew up with a different script, they might well retain their right-left and their clockwise sequences. We shall return to this in the next chapter.

PAIRED AND RADICAL SEQUENCES

When a human is drawn with a circle and four sticks, in what order are the sticks drawn? Do children proceed around the circle? Or do they break the four into two pairs, each left-right or right-left? To keep the drawings constant in form, we shall take 33 of the original 40, the 33 in which the arms are drawn out of the 'head' rather than out of the 'neck' or 'legs'. Among these 33, 14 were radial (that is, drawn around the circle) and 19 paired. An example of each of the four possible orders is shown in (25): radial clockwise and counter-clockwise; paired right-left or left-right.

Radial and paired orders are interesting as examples of the way a series of actions may form a small 'chunk' or, in Kevin Connolly and Jerome Bruner's terms, a 'sub-routine'. Each pencil stroke, each body part, is no longer an isolated act but is bound into a small series that can be regarded as a unit of activities in its own right. How do such 'chunks' – radial or paired – get formed?

Radial orders remind one of Rhoda Kellogg's argument that humans often evolve out of 'sun' drawings. Perhaps this evolution applies to sequence as well as to form: radial drawings tended to be produced more often by younger children in our

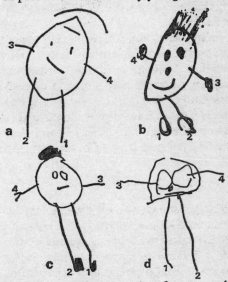

(25)   Radial and paired constructions for arms and legs.

group, although we would need more drawings to be sure that this was consistently true of all children.

If radial orders are the earliest form, what gives rise to paired orders? Practice in drawing could be a factor, but it doesn't seem so from the drawings we have. For instance, (25*d*) strikes one as a shaky and inexperienced drawing, but the sequence was paired. In contrast (25*b*) has more sureness and verve, but the sequence was radial. Perhaps we need to keep in mind several possible factors: practice with shapes, some general body-concepts, or the beginnings of general concepts about left and right.

TOP-TO-BOTTOM ORDERS

Of the 79 children, 68 started with an initial circle. Sequencing of this sort does appear to be affected by experience. We know from studies made over long periods, like Helga Eng's, that the first humans children produce do not always start at the top.[2] We also know, from Marcia Bernbaum's observations in Honduras, that unschooled children aged seven to eleven, working with an unfamiliar medium (a pencil) and asked to copy a complex geometric shape, show at first no consistent top-bottom pattern.[3] So when a child starts at the bottom or the middle of a human, we may suspect lack of experience. Though then again, the strategy may be deliberate: humans started from the bottom will certainly have leg-room.

What happens after the initial circle? Here there are two separate sequences we need to distinguish. First, sequences that are completely top-to-bottom, with no returns up the figure (circle and face details; trunk with arms; then legs and feet). We can call these 'finish as you go along'. Secondly, sequences that are top-to-bottom but also include returns to add extra details (circle, eyes, legs, return for hair or arms). In these sequences the strategy is 'go back to finish'.

The difference between these strategies is important for a very simple reason. The items one must return for are the ones likely to be forgotten – just as we ourselves do not always return to the top of the house, the first parts of the garden, or the early parts of a problem. Returning to details means that we have to overcome the sense of having finished. It also means that we have become adept at monitoring, at running a critical eye over a finished piece of work to see if all the pieces are there that should be there. And for this, we shall in turn need either a fairly clear image of what the finished work should look like, or else an effective list for checking off items.

How does this point apply to children's drawings? To return to our 79 children, 50 of them used this sequence: circle, some face details, then legs. Of these 50, 21 then stopped so these accounted for half of the 39 armless humans. The others returned up the figure to add arms or other facial features (mouth, nose, ears, hair, glasses). Of all items, however, arms tended to be at the end of the list. They were in fact the absolutely last item for 28 of the 40 children who included arms.

Why are arms so often the last item? The reason is far from clear. Arms are perhaps the item that belong least clearly to the important vertical stem and, once they are no longer a part of a radial order or some other construction system that brings them in effortlessly, they require a monitoring effort that children do not make. Two things we can be sure of, however: first, armless humans reflect no strange perception on the part of a child; instead they may often simply reflect the sense of having finished by the time one reaches the bottom; secondly, the phenomenon of no-return is not limited to young children only. As we saw in chapter 2, older children also often omit arms or hands once they begin to use embracing lines to join parts of a figure (15). Any parts not included within the embracing line become 'extras', putting them in requires a return to an earlier point. This return is often not made.

FROM CORE TO ACCESSORIES

We can talk about 'core' and 'accessories' when we want to describe sequences with fairly large 'chunks' or units to them. We could, for example, describe a sequence in terms of each eye, each finger, each pair of limbs – but we might not gain much from this once we got beyond simple drawings. Instead, we might do better by using larger items for a sequence. Body and clothing, for instance, could form a sequence of two items.

Body and clothing are of special interest because of 'transparent' or 'X-ray' drawings, where the body is visible through the clothes. Such figures, often produced by children and by artists in 'primitive' cultures, run counter to a convention we seldom question – the convention that we include in a picture only what is visible. With 'primitive' artists, we can assume that the convention is not followed, and may ask ourselves: why should it be? With children in our own culture, though, more complicated explanations have been offered. To some psychologists transparencies are a sign of impulsivity and immaturity. But one might simply say that children commonly start with a standard body and then add clothes without erasing the underlying body. (These two explanations of course are not completely incompatible. An 'impulsive' child may be one who tends not to plan ahead, not to anticipate a final result. The same may be said, however, of a retarded child.)

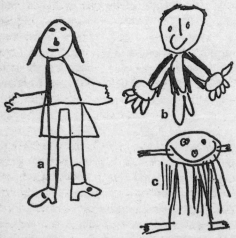

(26) Three frequent solutions to the problem of drawing a person with a long coat: (*a*) 'outline', (*b*) 'line-on-line', (*c*) 'scribble over'.

Belle Mann and Elyse Lehman recently asked what happens when children are asked to draw figures that might invite transparencies, such as 'a lady with a long skirt', or 'a man who's wearing a coat because it's cold outside'.[4] They were interested both in the sequencing and in the final product.

The request for clothes did in fact produce a large number of transparencies: roughly one third of nearly two hundred drawings produced by children between four and nine. The three most frequent types were: first, superimposed 'outlines' as in (26a) (these accounted for 67 per cent of all cases); secondly 'line-on-line', as in (b); and thirdly 'scribble', as in (c). In terms of age, 'scribble' was most common among the younger children, 'line-on-line' was next on the age scale, and 'outline' predominated at the end. Regardless of type, the sequence was always body first and clothes later.

How else might children get round this problem? A variety of their solutions is shown in (27), collected during a pilot study by Belle Mann[4]. In each pair, the drawing on the left was a response to the request to 'draw a person'. The drawing on the right was a response to a later request to 'draw a person with a long skirt'. In pairs (a) and (b) the original figure has simply been elongated; in pairs (c) to (g), the clothing has been fitted either inside or outside the original figure. In pairs (h) and (i), the clothing has been outlined over the original; in pair (j) the clothing has been effectively added to a modification of the original shape.

How do children feel about their X-ray solutions? Are they content? Or are they concerned about departing from the Western convention that drawings normally include only what is visible from one point of view? Many of the children observed by Belle Mann and Elyse Lehman were dissatisfied with their drawings and added explanatory comments: references to 'grass skirts', 'see-through skirts', or 'long hair' (for a scribble-over solution). These children clearly sensed there was a

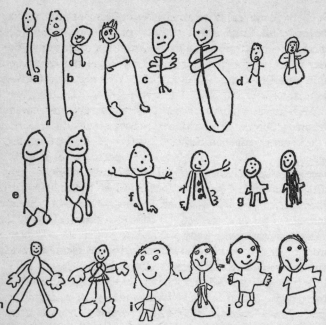

(27) Drawing a person with a long coat or skirt. The left-hand drawing in each pair shows a child's usual rendering of a person; the right-hand drawing shows the same child's drawing of person plus clothing.

problem to be solved. Most of them, however, did not see that the adult solution called for advance planning, or else they were unable to make the major modification required in the core of their standard figures.

CONSTRAINED DRAWINGS

When we ask children to draw something new, for instance 'a lady with a long skirt', we are working on the assumption that a particular kind of sequence will occur and will create a problem.

Suppose, however, that we wish to make more sure that a particular sequence does occur or that we want to see the effect of one particular unit in a sequence on other units. We may wait until children spontaneously produce this particular unit. Or alternatively, we may start the drawing and ask children to complete it.

What kinds of effects can be investigated with constrained drawings? We will be considering two effects here:

(a) *Fitting into the available space*. Once a first unit occupies space, later units must either be layered on top of it or, to have their own space, be fitted into whatever is left. This is the effect made familiar by the poster 'THINK AHEAD'. Fitting activities into available time or purchases into a limited budget, often display the same constraints.

(b) *Agreements with earlier units*. For any activity to display order or consistency, later steps need some degree of fit with what has gone before. Different individuals, though, will have different ideas about 'fit'. For our purposes, what we need to explore then are the individual definitions of reasonable fit or agreement. What do children, for example, regard as a reasonable fit between an early and a later part of a drawing? What are the principles they follow in accepting some later units as feasible and others as not? And do their views about reasonable fit help account for the drawings they produce?

PHYSICALLY AVAILABLE SPACE

Within children's free drawings, we can easily observe some end-effects due to running out of space: effects such as minimal legs, or bent arms that go down to the bottom and then up the side of the page. We can also begin to unravel some oddities such as the fact that schoolchildren, both in the USA and in Japan,[5] usually draw trains moving to the left. This is probably because the engine is typically drawn first, at the left, and the rest of the train can move in no other direction. (See (28) for two examples from US children, different in complexity but similar in direction.)

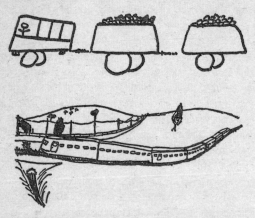

(28) Two trains. In both drawings, overall direction of movement is decided by the fact that the engine was drawn first – to the left.

Available space might also account for the positions children often give to details of a drawing. There are times when their placement of body details, such as facial features of the human in (29a), seem to reflect the intention they had at the beginning of the drawing: in this case the intention to make the large single circle stand for head and trunk combined. In similar fashion the buttons of (b) seem well-placed. At other times, though. the position of details such as the large 'stomach' drawn inside the lady of (c), or the stripes 'from neck to feet' in our terms (d) seem to reflect less an intention to render positions or proportions realistically and more an aesthetic or playful response to the fact that the space is there.

In pursuit of further data, we asked the 79 children who had drawn circle-plus-stick humans to add one final detail for

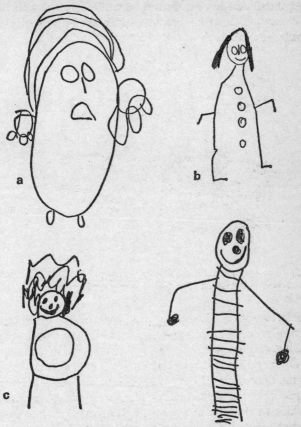

(29) Details inside the frame of a figure; in (a) and (b) placement seems to reflect realistic proportions and may be intentional, but in (c) and (d) it seems to be mainly decided by available space.

us, either a 'stomach' (or, for the many children who looked blank at the word 'stomach', a 'belly-button'). This was a detail unlikely to have been part of the plan with which they had started their drawings. The position of the belly-button turned out to depend on the relative sizes of the circle and the 'leg' sticks. When the circle was longer, the belly-button was usually placed within it, but where the sticks were longer, the button was usually placed between them. Some examples are shown in (30).

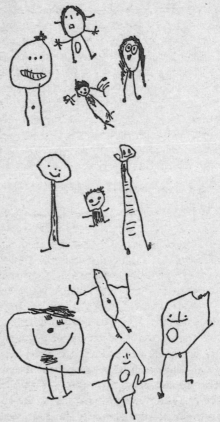

(30) Placement of the belly-button may reveal whether circle or sticks represent the trunk.

Results of this sort highlight the possibility that children can regard a circle they draw as standing for both head and trunk (a reasonable idea), or the sticks they draw as standing for both trunk and legs (an equally reasonable idea). They may in fact not even choose between these two possibilities until fitting in an extra detail forces a choice, a choice affected by the relative amounts of space available. Regrettably, children's plans or intentions at the start of a drawing are difficult to pin down. Probably the best that we adults can do is to be aware that children's plans may change, and that they may use units to depict meanings in ways that we ourselves would not. We should be reluctant to assume that our own concepts about the right way to indicate head and trunk are the same as the child's, or better than a child's. Above all, we should be reluctant to say, as people often say, 'You've left out its body,' or something of that sort.

AGREEMENTS WITH EARLIER UNITS

Looking at free drawings, Sarah Friedman and I noted a number of 'slanted' humans (31) and began to suspect that an accidentally slanted intitial circle had led to these.[6] Once the circle was drawn, then the eyes were drawn on an axis that fitted with the circle slant, and so forth. To test this idea, we gave children an incomplete figure; a single circle in the centre of the page, with two dots close to one side, or two dots close to the usual 'jaw-line' (32 and 33). If these beginnings are effective constraints, children should produce for us more sideways or upside-down humans than usual. In fact this is what they did. And especially interesting are the ways in which they coped with the incomplete figure we gave them. There are actually two possible constraints: first, the need to establish some agreement among parts of the body, for example by arranging them all along the same axis, or placing the different facial features at reasonable distances from one another.

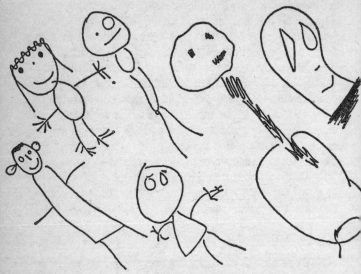

(31) A variety of slanted humans. The angle of the initial unit (top circle) seems to set the angle for the remainder.

Secondly, the convention – in our society – that the bottom of the page represents the ground.

Take first the case where dots were close to the bottom of the circle (32). The problem could have been solved by ignoring the second constraint, simply letting the figure be, on our standards, 'upside-down'. And indeed, for some young children this constraint might not even exist, since they might not have learned to equate the bottom of the page with the ground. But most of the children we worked with certainly were aware of the difficulty: many asked if they could turn the page and some, when asked to try without turning, said the problem was impossible – 'You can't do it.'

Children who are taking agreement along a common axis as the major principle, though, will draw their figures upside-

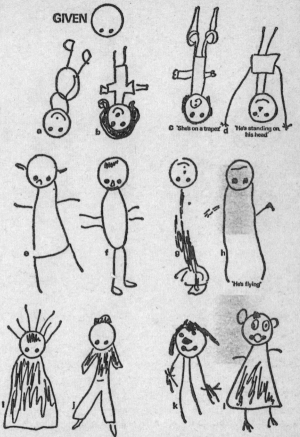

(32) How children complete a figure whose eyes have already been drawn low in the circle.

down, either without comment or else legitimized as 'standing on their hands' or 'hanging from a trapeze'. If they are drawing 'right-side-up', they may cope with the awkward eyes by omitting the mouth or by squeezing it into its usual place

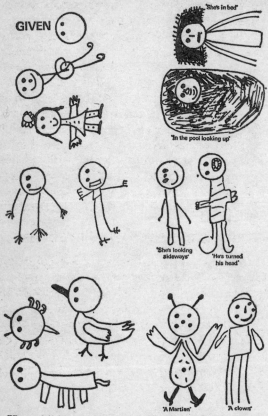

(33) How children complete a figure whose eyes have already been placed sideways in the circle.

regardless of proportion. Alternatively, children may split the figure, keeping eyes and mouth in agreement within the head, but nonetheless orienting torso and legs to the bottom of the page. In our group these split figures were always given some special explanation: 'He's flying,' or 'She has her head way back.' The third possibility is the most ingenious: this is to adopt a solution that meets all constraints by altering the initial unit ($32k$ and l). The children have essentially redefined the problem. These solutions, incidentally, are not always those of the older children. For instance, (l) was made by one of the youngest children, at just over four-and-a-half.

In (33) are the solutions we got for the half-drawn face where the eyes were side-on. In addition to the other solutions, the drawings show a particular kind of redefinition that we only saw with end-on eyes, namely conversion to animal figures. This conversion in itself seems to overcome the usual assumption that the completed figure should be human (though in fact the instructions we gave were neutral: 'Somebody else started this drawing and didn't finish it: could you?')

LIMITS TO THE EFFECTS OF EARLIER UNITS

How far do units drawn first affect later ones? The strength of the effect might be expected to vary with the type of unit. Do eyes, for instance, exert more pull than arms? Which have the most effect? Alternatively, the degree of effect might vary from one child to another: we have already seen, for example, that there are marked differences in the way children respond to a unit half drawn for them. In this next section, we explore some material on limits related to the nature of the unit and the nature of the child.

LIMITS RELATED TO THE TYPE OF UNIT.

How children respond to eyes drawn on a strange axis indicates one way in which a unit early in the sequence can affect a later one: the early unit affects the orientation of the later unit because of an accepted need to arrange all the separate units along a common axis.

How far will children depart from their usual orientation?

We are, after all, working with a phenomenon – people 'upside-down' or 'lying down' – that is not unusual in children's spontaneous drawings. Could we produce an orientation that is less usual? In addition, can we find an effect on the *form* of a later unit as well as on its orientation? If a figure is given one arm, for example, will children tend to draw in the other arm even when they are of an age at which many children omit arms altogether? If the given arm is drawn as a stick and at a 45 degree angle to the body, will the other arm (and perhaps the legs as well) be drawn in similar fashion? Or will children retain their own preferred types of unit?

To answer this question, Nona Flynn, Roslyn Dawes and I adapted for completion a drawing originally used by Frances Ilg and Louise Ames.[7] All the drawings shown in (34) are completions of this one. The advantages of the figure (overcoming its lack of charm) lie in its unusual arm angle and its strange hand structure. Both of these face children with a choice between, on the one hand, following their usual preferences (arm at 90 degrees; no fingers – or at any rate fingers unlike these) and, on the other, having the limbs agree in type.

These completions were gathered by Nona Flynn in Washington, DC and by Roslyn Dawes in Sydney. In both countries, most of the children were four-, five- or six-year-olds (in nursery school or kindergarten), and the collections turned out to be very similar. First, when one arm and hand are given, all children add a counterpart, even though they do not often include arms and hands in their spontaneous drawings. Secondly, they solve the conflict between given arm and usual arm in a variety of ways: some children just draw arms and legs in their own manner, regardless; some match the given arm either in form or orientation; some match it in both; and in some cases the given arm has an effect on both arms and legs (34h) but this is rare. Most of the solutions we got were of the first two types, and younger children generally showed

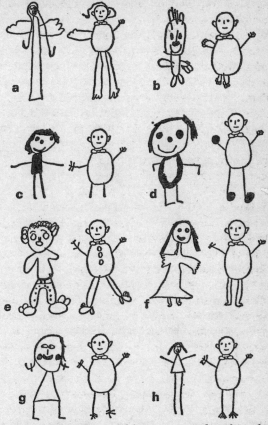

(34)   Completing a figure with one arm and no legs: how the arm influences the rest.

more resistence both to the form and orientation of the given arm than older children. This resistance is of special interest since it occurs at the same age (four and early five) that shows a particular insistence on agreement, in the sense that for these

children it is most important that body parts (head, trunk, legs)
should fall along the same axis.

All in all, the arm completions leave one with the feeling
that there are limits to how much effect an earlier unit can have
and that some earlier units have a stronger role than others.
What earlier units have the strongest effects? At hunch level,
we might expect that units seldom omitted (such as eyes)
or drawn first (like the initial circle) will exert more influence
than those which are often left out or drawn last (such as
arms or hair).

LIMITS RELATED TO DIFFERENCES AMONG CHILDREN.

At any age, children clearly differ in the ingenuity with which
they evade a constraint or insist upon producing their usual
formula figures. It would be interesting to know if these
aspects of insistence or ingenuity apply only to graphic work
or are more general characteristics.

As it is, we have little date on these individual differences.
One interesting piece of information, though, is provided by
Norman Freeman, who asked children of three and four to
complete a series of drawings, all without arms and all composed of two circles: a head with facial features, and a trunk.[8]
The sizes of the head and trunk were varied systematically:
sometimes they were equal, sometimes the head was larger,
sometimes the trunk. All children added the legs to the trunk,
but how they placed the arms varied according to the types
of drawing they normally produced. The children for whom
the given units had the least effect were the older ones
(four-year-olds) who usually drew figures consisting of two or
more circles ('conventional' figures). The children affected
most tended to be the younger ones (three-year-olds) who
usually drew figures composed of one circle only, plus two or
four sticks. For these children, 'the larger the head in relation to
the trunk the greater the tendency to draw arms on to the head'.

In effect, earlier units only had this particular consequence when children were working with a figure not of the type they usually drew – a figure that was in fact one step beyond what they usually drew. It may be that some earlier units have maximum effect in the climate of uncertainty that surrounds working in new areas.

SOME UNANSWERED QUESTIONS

We clearly have much to learn about the differential effects of particular units in a sequence, and about the differences among individuals in their susceptibility to constraints – to the initial premises of a graphic problem. These questions are not unanswerable: it is simply a matter of choosing which question to work on first.

A second set of answerable questions revolves around the possibility that some sequential features are not limited first to drawings of people. The tendency to proceed from top to bottom and from left to right, for example, appears to apply as well to the way we construct letters of the alphabet and geometric shapes. If this were so, then it would appear that some aspects of sequence apply to a wide variety of shapes and have some general basis. It might also be that sequence is helpful in accounting for the errors children so often produce in copying geometric shapes and letters.

To explore such possibilities, we need a variety of shapes. They should be simple, so that we can easily observe the sequence. They should also be uniform – we need to avoid the variety of figures that people beyond the age of three or four can produce if left to their own devices. Asking people to copy set geometric or letter-like designs cuts down the variety, makes the sequence easy to observe, and allows the possibility of errors that approximate errors with the alphabet. The sequences people follow – and the effects of sequence – are described in the next chapter.

4 Copying simple shapes

At first glance, copying geometric and letter-like shapes may seem rather dull compared with drawing human figures. But in fact the task has a number of features – both in real life and in experimentation – that make it rewarding.

(a) *To begin with: the skill has practical consequences.* Most children face the task of copying letter shapes, a task that calls for scanning a shape, putting together a set of strokes, and meeting expectations that may vary from 'a recognizable letter' to 'a pleasant hand'. In the process, they may also be asked to copy geometric shapes. These are often used as a preliminary to printing, and printing itself used as a preliminary to cursive writing, although the value of and the reasons for this sequence are still debated. In a more clinical setting, copying geometric shapes is also often included in psychological tests, where it is intended to serve as an indicator of perceptual-motor maturity or – in some cases – of brain damage.

(b) *The path is often stressed by teachers.* In the English-writing world, for instance, children are not usually let loose with letters of the alphabet. Instead, they are carefully shown where to start and which lines to draw first: in effect, they are given a path. In fact, a number of systems exist that demonstrate paths or that use paths as ways of grouping letters (for example, grouping all the letters that start with a stick on the left, or all the letters that start at a two o'clock position). The assumption behind all of these is that the correct path makes a difference to the letter produced: it helps avoid errors or produces a neater copy. In some other countries, however, letter-paths seem not to be thought so important. We were, for example, put to some trouble to find a book setting out paths for children to use in learning to write Hebrew, and most teachers of Hebrew – both in Israel and the USA – assured us that a careful prescription of paths was not a major issue in learning to write. Whether this difference in approach reflects a difference in the letters to be learned or in attitude towards learning, we do not know. But in neither culture is there much information about the paths children normally follow, especially when dealing with untaught shapes. Nor is there an abundance of firm data about relationships between specific letter-paths and problems children meet in learning to write.

(c) *Thirdly, copying provides a miniature model.* Psychology makes much use of 'simple' tasks that serve as helpful models of complex activities. The game of '20 Questions', for instance, serves as a model for hypothesis-testing in general, the games of 'O'Grady' or 'Simon says' as models for verbal control over movement. Copying in its turn is a miniature, a small model for several broader issues.

First, it provides a manageable way of exploring the effects of experience and the nature of the transfer of skills. The world is happily supplied with a variety of scripts, most written top-to-bottom, some left-to-right, others right-to-left. We might well ask just how much variety does exist, and why it exists. We may also ask: does experience with script transfer to copying other shapes? If so, is the effect the same at all ages or stronger at some ages than others?

Secondly, copying provides a small window on to the general development of consistency and flexibility in behaviour. It could be, for instance, that we learn to draw each shape separately, acquiring or exhibiting a new path each time. If so, we might be encouraged to think of behaviour in general as highly specific – with development occurring in piecemeal fashion. Alternatively, we might show consistency across shapes, as if we were following a set of rules or principles that could be extended to any new shape. If this were so, we might be encouraged to think of behaviour as highly consistent, with development marked by active abstraction and extension of general themes. To consider such large possibilities as universals requires many studies. We may add something to the accumulating pile of them by asking such questions as: do sequential patterns conform to some general rules that are more or less independent of the actual shapes being copied? Are the rules the same when we draw from memory, or when we vary the hand used? Do we use the same patterns all the time, or do we fit the cut to the cloth, the sequence to the shape or to our purpose?

Finally, copying is an attractive testing ground for ideas about the nature and basis of error. Copying is a task where errors abound, and where we already know a little about them. We know, for instance, that some shapes are more difficult than others: on the Binet intelligence test, 'reasonable' copies of a square are expected around five years, but 'reasonable' copies of a diamond are not expected until around seven. We also know that some errors (for instance, left-right reversals – *b* for *d*) are especially common. But we do not know why. Small wonder, then, that copying becomes an attractive area for working out ideas about the extent to which children pay attention to the orientation of shapes, or working out ideas about the relationships between 'perception' and 'production'. In brief, copying may tell us something not only about the nature of copying and writing, but also something about other aspects of behaviour.

This chapter deals with several aspects of sequential patterning, starting with ways of describing sequences and rules, leading on to a look at conditions that affect sequence (changes in the task, experience with script, right or left-handedness), taking a detour to look at some ways in which scripts vary around the world, and ending with the consequences of sequence, especially those consequences that we label 'errors'.

DESCRIBING SEQUENCES AND RULES

In (35) are shown a number of simple shapes and some paths or sequences widely used by children. (You may wish, before reading further, to cover over the paths and note your own sequence. Bear in mind, however, that adults are more variable or individual than six-year-olds).

Some paths used by children occur quite early. We found, for example, like Arnold Gesell and Louis Ames in 1946, that about 80 per cent of four-year-olds in nursery school drew the vertical line of a cross first, followed by the horizontal.[1] Other common paths come in at a later age. On the cross, for example, drawing the horizontal from left to right comes in later than drawing the vertical from top to bottom. In addition, some paths come in, reign for a few years, and then decline. Frances Ilg and Louise Ames found that the first path shown for the square in (35), for instance, builds up in frequency to become the most common among six-year-olds, and then drops off to half its former strength by age nine.[2]

Gesell and his associates – Ilg and Ames – were primarily concerned with locating typical patterns for particular shapes at different ages, with the eventual goal of using paths as one piece of information to help determine children's maturity and their readiness for school. Their work has yielded an enormous amount of meticulous data, and it gives us an idea of what to expect at a particular age level, at least in our society. It leaves us, however, with the task of finding a way of talking about paths in general or shapes *in general*. Without such a way, we

DESIGN	COMMON PATTERN (●=START)	% OF CHILDREN SHOWING EACH PATTERN (% OF CORRECT DRAWINGS)			% OF BOYS & GIRLS SHOWING EACH PATTERN			
		N	K	I		N	K	I
+					M	57	86	90
		79	88	89	F	92	91	89
|—					M	67	79	100
		71	88	100	F	75	100	100
					M	45	100	100
		71	91	95	F	100	82	89
					M	33	93	90
		63	88	90	F	92	82	89
					M	25	0	0
		12	4	0	F	0	9	0
					M	8	43	50
		33	52	69	F	58	64	89
					M	42	14	10
		21	7	5	F	0	0	0
					M	0	64	60
		25	68	52	F	50	73	44
					M	17	14	20
		25	16	37	F	33	18	56

(35) Some sample paths drawn by children of four to five, five to six, and six to seven, in the same school. At this school, sex differences (indicated by brackets) were rather marked.

shall be forever working with too many specific shapes, arguing constantly from individual cases.

Suppose we ask whether children follow some general 'rules'

or 'principles' – that is, whether they use sequential patterns that cut across a variety of shapes. Do children, for instance, generally start at the top, at the left, or with a vertical rather than a horizontal line? To the extent that they do, we have some evidence of consistency across shapes and also a tool that helps us rise above single shapes.

We see from (36) that consistency does exist: we can in fact chart the development of sequential rules across different ages, from nursery school to adulthood. For example, these starting rules: start at a topmost point, at a leftmost point, and with a vertical line. The first two of these grow increasingly strong with age, but the third varies more among adults than among children of around five. Not all rules, apparently, become firmer and firmer with age.

Three further rules apply to progressions beyond a starting point: draw all horizontal lines from left to right; draw all verticals from top to bottom, and 'thread' (follow a continuous line without a change in meeting point, as if you were laying out a thread). These rules often conflict with one another. To sense the conflict, try drawing a square. To use a continuous line, you must draw one horizontal left to right and one vertical from top to bottom. In effect, you must choose among rules. When children choose in this way, interestingly they prefer threading, and this preference increases in strength through our nursery school and kindergarten groups (groups 1 and 2 in (36)) and then declines. This rise and fall in threading is reminiscent of children's coming to use an embracing line (a continuous or near-continuous contour) in their human figure drawings: in both cases children move from discrete lines to greater continuity. Perhaps in both cases they are responding to some increasing awareness that shapes do form units and can be drawn as units. But we are actually far from knowing the basis of threading. In the USA, however, we may note an odd relationship between threading and school

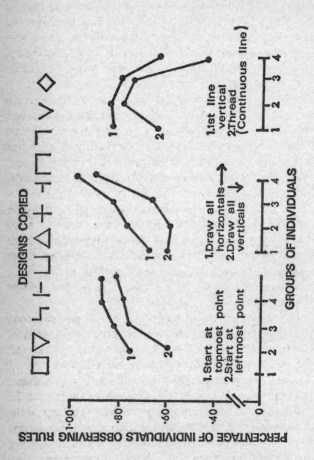

(36) Frequency with which six rules are followed by individuals in four groups: (1) four to five, (2) five to six, (3) six to seven, and (4) adult.

experience. Threading on our geometric shapes was strongest at a time when the children were being taught to print, in a school where cursive writing (which involves threading far more than printing does) was not introduced until they were eight. By then, however, to judge from Ilg's and Ames' data, threading is already on a decline, with very little remaining by around age nine.

Clearly we can describe sequential consistency by reference to a set of production rules. And we can chart the ups and downs of such rules in relation to a variable such as age.

We can also take two other steps. We can, first of all, begin to understand why children sometimes do unexpected things, like start drawing some shapes from the bottom rather than the top. If you are asked to draw an inverted U, for example, you will need to choose between starting at the top and threading. A shift among US children from top-starting to bottom-starting around the age of seven, for instance, does not indicate some sudden loss of an old pattern or the presence of whimsy. What is happening is that another rule (threading in this case) happens to be especially strong around this time. In the conflict, threading wins.

The second step is to begin looking at differences among shapes. Psychologists are still searching for useful ways of describing shapes, ways of specifying how they are like and unlike one another. Once we have a reliable statement of sequential rules, we can suggest that one way in which shapes differ is in terms of the rules that can apply to them. An L-shaped design, for instance, allows you to start at the top, at the left, and with a vertical stroke; it also allows you to thread and at the same time to draw the vertical from top to bottom and the horizontal from left to right. In brief, all the rules can be followed. In contrast, an inverted L-shape (⌐) forces you to make a choice among rules: you cannot, for instance, thread and start at the leftmost point. Shapes where rules conflict, or where the usual rules do not apply, may turn out to be the ones where children are least certain of what to do, most reluctant to try, most liable to error, or most likely to reject what they produce as somehow 'wrong' or 'unattractive'.

In brief, rules promise to be a useful way of looking at differences among shapes, and at the effect of conditions such as handedness or varying scripts. Two small caveats, however. One is that the rules mentioned here are not exhaustive. They are simply the rules that fit the shapes and the children I considered with Rochelle Levine in 1972.[3] We could easily add other rules. Young children of three or four, for instance, often start their copies from a junction of lines: the centre point of a cross or star is one example. And adults copying complex shapes may follow additional rules that relate to the way they break a figure into components and anticipate routes to a desired end result. The second caveat is that the term 'rule' does not imply that a person is aware of a principle and can state it. The term does imply, however, that consistency exists, that we can describe it, and that we can use it to begin predicting what might happen when an individual meets a new shape or starts a new task such as learning to write.

As a start, let us consider what happens when we begin to change the setting in which we look for sequential rules: changes in the task, in the hand used, and in the experience of learning to write. These changes help us find ways of describing patterns and of locating their sources.

VARIATIONS IN SEQUENTIAL PATTERN

Four conditions might well affect the extent to which a rule is followed. These are: first, the demands of the task, for example, training compared with copying or drawing from memory; secondly, a lack of experience with script; thirdly,

xperience with varying scripts (a condition calling for a detour
) look at differences among scripts); and last the hand used
)r copying.

HANGES IN THE TASK

Elyse Lehman, Marcia Bernbaum and I have tested the effect
)f several task changes. One of these changes is to ask children
) draw a shape from memory instead of copying it with the
hape present all the time. This tells us whether the sequential
pattern comes from something the eye is doing at the time of
drawing, and the answer is in fact that the same rules are
followed whether the copy is drawn from memory or the shape
emains present.

Suppose we ask children to trace over shapes, rather than
copy them on to a blank sheet. This does generate some
surprise. Most of the rules (such as starting at the top, or
hreading) apply with equal strength to both tasks. But
tarting at the left does not. Among US kindergartners who
opy shapes by starting at the left, tracing produces either no
preference for left-starting or else a preference for right-
tarting. Among second-graders, the two tasks elicit the same
)ehaviour. This kind of result tells us that a rule does not
pring full-grown from some central source, to be applied to
ll situations encountered. In addition, it suggests, on the
practical teaching scene, some caution in using tracing as a
preliminary for copying and printing, as has been done since
he time of the early Greeks. It may be that tracing does not
chieve the practice effects desired. Unless the path is specified,
eft to themselves, children may be happily practising some
path quite different from what we have in mind. And for those
hildren who do have a need to establish and practise a specific
path, the time and effort devoted to tracing may not be well
pent.

CHILDREN WITHOUT AN ALPHABET

What happens when children have not been taught to write?
Marcia Bernbaum asked this question for children in Honduras,
comparing seven-to-eleven-year-olds in school with children
of the same ages who had not attended school.[4] Two of her
results are of special interest:

(a) A great deal depends on the *familiarity of the shape*. When
copying with a pencil, for example, schooled and unschooled
children used the same strategies as long as the shape was
simple: 95 per cent of each group, for instance, started a
single horizontal line at the left and a single vertical line at the
top. With more complex shapes, however, such as a triangle or
the letter Z, the unschooled children showed no particular
preference for any strategy. On the letter Z, for example, some
started at the left, some at the right; some started at the top,
some at the bottom; some started with a horizontal line, some
with the diagonal.

(b) A great deal depends on the *familiarity of the medium*.
Marcia Bernbaum had the excellent idea of asking some of the
unschooled children to draw in the sand with a finger: she had
already noticed children drawing outlines in the sand for
hopscotch and other games. Using this technique, the unschooled children showed sequence strategies essentially the
same as those followed by the schooled. (The quality and
accuracy of the drawn shapes also improved dramatically.)
The moral, Bernbaum felt, was that teachers or parents need
to introduce graphic work from known shapes and known
media. The 'teacher should recognize that most . . . students
. . . come to school equipped with several basic skills necessary
for learning to write . . . (they) should seek media and figures
with which the children are already familiar and use them as a
stepping stone to the relatively unfamiliar writing situation'

CULTURAL VARIATIONS IN SCRIPT

Before we ask about agreements between the way geometric shapes are copied and letters are written, we need to understand something about scripts themselves and the way they vary. This side-step turns out to be fascinating as well as informative. It is not without reason that David Diringer subtitles his classic work on *The Alphabet*,* 'a key to the history of mankind'.[6] People have clearly long been eager to record words clearly. They have also been amazingly versatile in borrowing and inventing ways to do so. This historical interest is also made clear more briefly in Carol Donoghue's *The Development of Writing*.[7] Both books are a salutary reminder that shapes for writing may take a variety of forms, each 'natural' within its culture.

Is there, however, an indefinite number of ways in which shapes can be constructed, whatever their appearance? We need to distinguish carefully between two aspects of sequence:

(a) *The direction in which shapes succeed one another on the page*. This direction may be from left to right as in English, or from right to left as in Hebrew or Arabic. It may even be – as was the ancient Greek script called *boustrophedon* – written towards the left on one line and towards the right on the next. In addition, shapes may succeed one another down the page, as in traditional Chinese, or proceed up the page, as in a script called *batak*. Finally, the same direction may not apply to both letters and numbers. In both modern Arabic or Hebrew, for example, letters follow one another right-to-left, but all numbers with two or more digits and written left-to-right. On any one page, then, a pupil may need to switch direction.

*From which a good many of the data in the following pages derive

1	2	3	4	5	6	7	8	9	10
١	٢	٣	٤	٥	٦	٧	٨	٩	١٠

(37) A page of Arabic, illustrating the right-left progression of letters and left-right progression of numbers. Suggestion: try decoding the numbers and carrying out the problems.

There is by no means agreement among experts as to why one sequence occurs rather than another, although one frequent hypothesis concerns the nature of the medium – either the instrument used for writing, or the nature of the surface (stone, clay, porous paper). Diringer suggests, for example, that *batak* owes its unusual direction to the fact that it is written on strips of bamboo joined and folded in accordion-like fashion, and rotated for holding and reading purposes. In a less exotic fashion, stone has been thought to invite a right-to-left sequence, with the hammer held in the right hand and the chisel in the left, with the left arm obscuring some of the surface.

Not all aspects of sequence, however, seem to reflect the practicalities of the medium. Diringer reports some intriguing examples. With Egyptian hieroglyphics, for instance, 'the direction of writing was normally from left to right, the signs facing the beginning of the line . . .; sometimes, however, inscriptions were written from left to right, and sometimes, for purposes of symmetry, in both directions; in the latter cases, each of the two parts usually faces towards the centre, reading from there outwards'. Here 'art' seems to be a stronger influence than practicality. Equally appealing is the reasoning of Sultan Njoya of the Cameroons, who invented seven scripts from 1896 on: 'only the direction from right to left was to be avoided, because the neighbouring Haussa wrote in this direction, and it ought not to be thought that the script was borrowed from them'.

(2) *The direction followea in constructing an individual letter.* We might expect that Hebrew letters would be printed starting at the right, since the shapes succeed one another from right to left and the hand is moving from the right. In practice, however, this is not the case, as Sarah Friedman, Marcia Bernbaum Elyse Lehman and I learned to our surprise in a study with

ISRAELI PRINTING

Start at the top, at the left, with a horizontal stroke.

Given no top horizontal, start at the top and at the right.

Exceptions:

(38) Hebrew letters, grouped in terms of two rules for construction.

Israeli children.[8] Most letters are started at the left and the major differences from English printing are the tendency to start with a horizontal rather than a vertical stroke, and to draw 'o' shapes in clockwise fashion (38).

More data on sequences within shapes is needed from other cultures. We are told by Amia Lieblich and Amat Ninio, however, that cursive Arabic seems to differ from printed Hebrew: letters succeed one another from right to left and each shape is started at the right, yielding a nice homogeneity of experience.[9] We also know a little about Chinese, by courtesy of Eric Kvan of the University of Hong Kong, who reports that sequence is strongly emphasized, that letters are started at the top and at the left, but that, given two lines equally at the top, horizontal precedes vertical (39). Clearly, we have too little data to generalize from, but it might well be that directions within shapes show more consistency across cultures than do directions between shapes. There is, however, sufficient evidence to warrant our always looking separately at two aspects of sequence in a script: progression within a letter and progressions between letters.

EFFECTS FROM THE WAY INDIVIDUAL LETTERS ARE CONSTRUCTED

It would make good sense if single geometric shapes reflected the way individual letters are constructed rather than the sequence from one letter to another. And good sense does prevail. In Israel, for example, copies of single geometric shapes are usually started at the left, as most letters are. The right-to-left progression from one letter to the other seems to be irrelevant.

Is this the whole of the story, however? Do letters and geometric shapes always agree, at all ages? Here are some additional facts: children in the United States and Israel both

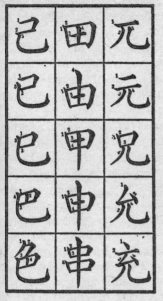
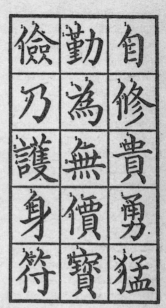

(39) A page of instructions for writing Chinese, illustrating attention paid to sequence and the way the same core shape appears in a variety of characters.

start drawing circles in a clockwise fashion. Around five to six, the US children switch to the anti-clockwise direction specified by most teachers of writing, and this switch is retained by most adults. In contrast, most Israeli children continue with the clockwise formation their teachers endorse.

US and Israeli children before school draw a cross with the vertical before the horizontal stroke. For a year or two after school begins, many Israeli children shift to drawing the horizontal first; they then revert to the original pattern. US children continue throughout with the pattern of vertical first.

C.D.—E

What happens with Arab children? Lieblich and Ninio report that Arab children in kindergarten generally draw a single horizontal line from left to right (75 per cent compared with an Israeli 95 per cent).[10] When they start school, however the percentage of Arab children using a left-to-right direction drops to 30 per cent. By second grade the percentage has dropped to 17 per cent and it stays low through to eighth grade.

From such data, three aspects of behaviour emerge. One is that some early sequences appear before learning to write and are not in agreement with the pattern of a script. The earlier pattern may be swamped by the later script but it did exist first. In effect, script will not turn out to be the only explanation for all sequential preferences.

The second is that we clearly need to distinguish among various rules or sequential preferences. Some of these – such as ways of drawing circular shapes – are highly malleable and can shift to fit with the demands of a script. Others – like starting at the top and, to a lesser extent, starting at the left – seem to be more constant: they occur in all scripts and in copying at an age before script is learned. From these preferences we might well suspect that the direction used – either for letters or geometric shapes – stem from some common underlying factor.

The third is that the effect of script often seems to be strongest close to the time of learning to write. It may well be true of all learning that we apply rules most rigidly and generalize most broadly at the time of first learning: behaviour that may be part of the danger of 'a little knowledge'.

EFFECTS FROM THE PROGRESSION
OF LETTERS ACROSS THE PAGE

There is, unfortunately, little data on relationships between letters and graphic work. Wayne Dennis and Evelyn Raskin report that the placement of a single figure drawing on a page varies with the sequence between letters (for example, more to the left in cultures with left-right sequence).[11] It would be interesting to know, in addition, whether pictures containing more than one figure are constructed differently in varying cultures. We do, however, have some tantalizing pieces of data on other performances. When children name pictures on a page, for example, they are most likely to do so from left to right in the USA or from right to left in Israel around the time when they are first learning to read. At this time, they impose the letter-order even on arrangements where it is difficult to sustain – such as a triangular array of pictures – suggesting once again that the developmental course is from applying a rule willy-nilly to applying it in moderation.

A similar course is suggested in Lila Ghent Braine's report of the way Israeli students (from primary school to college) arrange pictures on a page to tell a story or cancel out letters and numbers (for example cancel all 'a's' or all 'z's' on a page).[12] The data are complex and deserve close analysis. For our present purposes, however, we may note just one facet of special interest, namely the use by many Israeli college students of a *boustrophedon* order in cancelling letters and numbers. Apparently, when your culture requires you to work sometimes in one direction (Hebrew letters) and sometimes in another (numbers, music, English alphabet), you are most likely to develop a flexible variety of ways of working, choosing whatever seems most efficient for the occasion.

HANDEDNESS

People who write with the left hand are of constant interest: to psychologists, teachers, parents, and tool-makers as well as people interested in sequential patterns. They catch the general eye because they are visibly different. They have, for years, been suspected of being more awkward, less mature, more negativistic, and – most unjustifiably – likelier to have problems in reading. It is no accident that the word 'sinister' is the Latin for 'left'.

Left-handers (defined here as people who *write* with the left hand) catch the teacher's and the research worker's eye for two other reasons. One is that they do appear to have more problems in learning to write, especially 'a pleasant hand'. The other is that their spontaneous directional patterns may be different from those of right-handers. If so, we might have a clue to problems in writing, and a clue to one basis for sequential patterns, namely something about the hand and the way it is used.

Where should we look for effects? It is possible that the hand we use affects the way letters succeed one another on the page. We have no direct data on this, however. Indirectly, we may note that there are many cultures where shapes succeed one another in right-to-left fashion, but these do not appear to be 'left-handed' cultures: the percentage of left-handers typically falls between 5 and 10 per cent of any population.

In contrast, we do have one observation by Arnold Gesell and Louise Ames, to the effect that left-handers are more likely to start at the right of a shape than at the left, and at the bottom rather than the top.[13] Elyse Lehman and I asked children in matched pairs, (matched in the sense that each pair – one left-handed, one right-handed – attended the same kindergarten, helping us cut down any differences from teaching) to copy out single shapes.[14] Within such pairs, the only significant difference was in the frequency of starting at the left rather than at the right of a shape. Left-handers were far more likely to start at the top right of shapes such as rectangles, or to draw horizontal lines from right to left, or to draw down the right side of a triangle before the left. There were no other important differences. Handedness, then, is related only to one aspect of sequence (starting left or right) and cannot account for other aspects such as starting at the top, or threading. We shall have to look elsewhere for explanations of these.

In the meantime, what should we do with or for left-handers? One thing we might do is to channel our main efforts into the sequence that really counts, namely the sequence of letters across a page. When you write 'THE', for instance, the succession of letters across the page – 'THE' as against 'EHT' – is more important than whether individual lines are started at the left or the right. (This channelling of effort might be specially easy if we allowed left-handers to continue with print rather than shifted them to cursive). As a rule, unfortunately, left-handers are often given a great deal of practice in starting everything at the left, with the goal of developing a 'constant' left-right orientation on geometric and letter shapes, both within and between shapes. But around the world, millions of people manage without such constancy, so demanding it of left-handers seems unnecessary, especially as it goes against their particular grain.

Finally, since questions about left-handers are perennial, let me draw the attention of readers to what is generally agreed upon as important: first, that the paper should be placed at an angle that matches the angle of the arm, \ for right-handers, / for left-handers (a piece of tape on the desk will serve as a reminder, especially for children whose neighbours are right-handed). Secondly, that an upright or backhand slant should be tolerated.

THE CONSEQUENCES OF SEQUENCE

Sequences are interesting to observe. But are they more than just examples of the route children take in development? Should we, in a practical world, take them seriously? Is there any clear information on relationships between the way a simple shape is drawn and the kind of shape produced?

PAGE-TURNING

Children appear to rotate a drawing surface so that they can leave a hand movement undisturbed. In effect, the page shifts rather than the hand. With this observation in mind, Roslyn Dawes and I asked about 100 Australian children (aged three to six) to trace over a cart-wheel shape with four cross-lines creating eight spokes radiating out from the centre. The total circle was approximately four inches in diameter. We were intrigued to find that the number of turns increased rather than decreased with age, and that the direction of the turns was consistently one that would allow a stroke that ran from top to bottom, perpendicular to the bottom axis of the page. The final effect was in fact a clearer tracing – straighter lines – than if the child left the page-angle constant and drew more oblique lines. In brief, the page-turning was not a weird or irrational phenomenon but a neat case of problem-solving.

ERRORS IN SHAPE

Some time ago, Charlotte Rice noticed that if young children drew diamonds with one continuous line, the diamond was a poorer shape than if they used several separate lines.[15] Presumably, the use of several lines allows all lines to be drawn top-to-bottom and more accurately.

Ilg and Ames have also noted a type of error they call a 'closure' error, meaning an error in the region of drawing a figure to a close.[16] I have come to call these errors 'budget' problems: the difficulty is one of 'making ends meet'. In (40) there are a number of examples with triangles, including a dramatic example of difficulty with an inverted triangle intended to be South America (*e*).

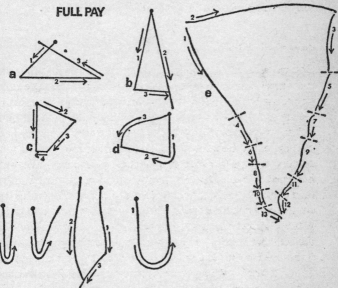

FULL PAY

(40) Examples of errors related to sequence. Drawings (*a*) to (*e*) illustrate problems of closure, of 'making ends meet'. Drawings marked (*f*) are copies of the letter V: the difficulties stem from starting with a perpendicular line.

With the inverted triangle, the difficulty stems from producing strokes that should be oblique but are too much like up and down strokes. Such a tendency should lead to trouble with letters such as V and in fact it often does. A number of attempts by Kindergarten children are shown in (40*f*). All of these errors combine a preferred stroke with a problem of anticipation. One suspects that improvement follows both from greater facility with oblique strokes and also from a greater readiness and ability to look ahead. As adults, we may be able to help children improve by being alert for letters or shapes that depart from the usual pattern of starting with an easy perpendicular line.

ERRORS IN ORIENTATION

Changes in the orientation of a shape fascinate both psychologists and educators for several reasons. First of all, a change in orientation sometimes has consequences: an inverted 'N' may be called 'wrong' or 'perceptually immature'; a reversed 'b' may be read as if it were 'd' and as a result not be understood.

From another point of view, reversals or rotations raise the question: what do young children attend to? Are they primarily sensitive to form, and initially indifferent to orientation which they acquire slowly (from maturation and school experience)? Or are they from the beginning sensitive to both form and orientation, so that most of their learning deals only with discovering when orientation counts, or what the meanings of various orientations are? (Children have to learn, for example, that one orientation on a page means that something is 'upside-down', another means 'lying down', and a third means 'bending'.) Psychologists are still working through the question of 'original indifference' *versus* 'original interest'. For the moment, we may note that the current balance is towards 'original interest' theories. We may also note that there seems to be a strong human tendency to label as 'indifference' any behaviour that consists of not paying attention to something in the same way that we do ourselves – whether that behaviour concerns shapes, manners, material property, dress, respect for age, or whatever. Many teenagers, for instance, have been mistakenly regarded as 'indifferent' to dress or appearance when the truth is they pay a great deal of attention to these, but to different features or on different occasions from those considered important by parents. The same human tendency often seems to be at work when people infer from children's graphic 'errors' that they are 'indifferent' to the orientation of shapes.

But on the other hand if young children are not indifferent to orientation, why do they produce the errors they do? One possibility is that no one has yet told them that the orientation of a shape sometimes makes a difference to what we call it. We call a person by the same name whether they stand up, lie down, bend over, or stand on their head. In fact, calling these shapes by the same name is regarded as an achievement, a recognition of equivalence or identity. But we call by different names the shape 'b' depending on its orientation. Riki Koenigsberger has in fact found that one of the quickest ways to produce an improvement in many children's judgements of 'b' and 'd' is to be very explicit about the rules of this particular game: to say and to demonstrate that for this shape the name does change when the orientation changes.[17]

A second possibility is that children are carried away by their preferred sequences, ending up in error on those shapes that require a change in their usual pattern.

We can, for example, easily see how this might happen with a letter such as 'N'. If one starts at the top left and uses a continuous line, the end result is '𝓝'. Less obvious is what happens with shapes such as '⊣' and '⊢'. One of these shapes (the second) produced more left-right reversals than the other in studies with pre-schoolers.[18]

It looks as though children reverse ⊣ and ⊢ because they tend to start at the left with a vertical stroke and then continue towards the right. If that is so we might expect them to reverse the letter 'd' more often than the letter 'b', and according to Edward and Hilda Lewis, they do.[19] Where children are taught to print by starting with 'a stick', the difference in frequency between 'b' and 'd' reversals might be especially marked.

It is not only within individual shapes, incidentally, that orientation can change as a result of sequence. It may happen as well to the way shapes follow one another. In (41) for instance, the child's reversed name was produced by starting at the right-hand side of the page. Note the way that individual letters also change from what is usual, and compare it with

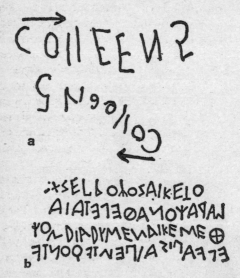

(41)   Letters may change in orientation, depending on whether they start at the left or the right side of a line. The names in (*a*) were written on separate occasions by a five-year-old; one started at the left of the page, the other at the right. The script in (*b*) is an example of *boustrophedon*, whose lines alternate in direction.

similar changes that occur in the example beside it of *boustrophedon* script, where the starting point of each line varies from line to line.

SEQUENTIAL PATTERNS AND TEACHING

Parents and other educators might well pay attention to sequence. First, they might note the double aspect (sequences between shapes and within shapes). If letters are produced neatly and progress as they should across the page (left to right for English), then the exact path for writing each letter should not be worried over. Our seventeen-year-old, for instance, has always drawn the letter 'O' by starting from the bottom and proceeding in clockwise direction. To me, his way of writing looks 'unnatural' and 'awkward', and I am tempted to interfere. But the letter is actually neat and the sequence of letters across the page is not affected. So I leave well enough alone.

Secondly, when errors do occur, it is as well to check the sequence. Suppose, for example, that a child writes his or her name in reversed fashion. The explanation may lie in starting at the right of the page rather than the left. A simple mark at the left will serve as a reminder, and may save a great deal of concern about deep sources of difficulty.

Does this mean that we should all pay careful attention before children even start drawing shapes, so that we can steer them from the beginning into particular paths? The evidence does not warrant this. Whole cultures, for example, manage quite effectively with scripts other than ours and paths other than ours. The wiser course appears to be one of recognizing that paths are likely to be more important on some shapes (the 'irregular' ones) than on others, and more important for some children (those who seem to have poor skills in breaking down shapes) than others.

We need to know far more about differences among children. Some children seem to be at ease with shapes, able to break them down and convert them comfortably into a series of actions. In contrast, I have seen children gaze at shapes as if they were impossible puzzles, wondering where to begin on the job of translating a completed pattern into something they should do. For these children, advice on paths to follow is extremely helpful. I have seen, for instance, one kindergartner successfully teach another how to draw a house by detailing the path: 'you start here and go down here and up here, and so on', instructions faithfully repeated by his friend as he produced his first successful drawing of a house. Similarly, Marcia Bernbaum found a description of paths a quick way of teaching unschooled children in Honduras how to produce accurate shapes and letters with the unfamiliar medium of a pencil.[20] Knowing the path seems to take care of at least some of the unknowns, so that it is possible to get started on the acquisition of a skill. Later on, the same end may be reached by a variety of routes. But in the beginning a set pattern cuts down anxiety and confusion, where they exist. Most drivers in a strange city will recognize this phenomenon, although here again there are some people who can strike out freely from the beginning and others who take a very long time to start venturing away from the known path.

One might expect some interaction between these two factors – that a tendency to 'maverick' or 'irregular' shapes might link up with some individual differences in children. Two studies point in this direction. One is a study by Robert Serpell, who found that orientation errors lasted until an older age among Zambians than among children in the UK or in the USA, especially reversals of shapes presented in a position that seemed 'wrong-side-up' in the children's own judgement.[21] The Zambian children, Serpell felt, had received less emphasis in their schooling on the need to be alert for orientation and had had less practice in monitoring their work – in constantly and carefully comparing it with the original.

The second study is by Minrie Abercrombie and her colleagues, R. L. Lindon and M. C. Tyson.[22] The shapes they asked children to draw were pairs of oblique lines, some placed parallel to one another (// or \\), some placed in opposing directions (/ \ or \ /). The parallel lines are the 'irregular' shapes, at least when, as in this case, they are drawn by simultaneous movement of the two hands because they run counter to the tendency to make one hand's line a mirror image of the other, to draw lines in opposing directions. Abercrombie found that for all children the 'irregular' shapes produced more errors than the 'regular' shapes; the difference was especially pronounced, however, among brain-injured children, who are often thought to have difficulty in monitoring or inhibiting a spontaneous action.

One should of course not conclude that all children who fail to be alert for irregular shapes are brain-injured. But any condition that lowers our alertness to the need to vary a usual route or pattern – whether it is fatigue, worry, impulsiveness, lack of warning, lack of experience – may have the same effect.

THE ROLE OF PERCEPTION

I have been emphasizing the importance of the sequential pattern. Does this mean, however, that perception plays no part? To take a specific case, is the occurrence of orientation errors unrelated to the way things look to children?

Perception seems to play a role in two interesting ways. One stems from the intriguing way in which children regard some shapes as 'right-side-up' and others 'upside-down', without regard to adult conventions. Anyone who has ever heard a three- or four-year-old protest at the 'wrong' hanging of his or her art will recognize the strength of the conviction. The conviction stems, it appears, from the presence of a focal point in every shape and from children's feelings that the shapes are 'right-side-up' when the focal point is in the upper half of the design. A number of designs that young children regard as 'right-side-up' are shown in (42); they are taken from the work of Lila Ghent Braine who first noted and studied the phenomenon.[23] This sense of rightness spills into graphic work because it seems that children are inclined, when they copy shapes, to produce them 'right-side-up' even when the original has been presented 'upside-down'. This kind of orientation 'error' is not attributable to sequential pattern. It is as if we, as adults, had noted that the original was 'a tree, upside-down', and had reproduced the essence of the message, namely 'a tree'. Unless the context included some specific reminder that the 'upside-down' aspect was equally essential, leaving it out and drawing a normal 'tree' would be very sensible.

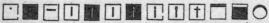

(42) Judgements of right-side-up: almost all children judge these figures to be right side up in the orientation shown here.

The other way in which perception probably plays a part lies in the tendency to confuse mirror images. A shape turned over on itself to left or right is less easily recognized as 'different' than a shape turned up or down on itself. This difference between inversions and left-right reversals appears to be based on something 'structural', on something in our visual system or central nervous system. As a result, we may always be somewhat prone to perceive mirror images as identical, and always be a little uncertain about whether a reversed shape has changed or not. Michael Cooke suggests that in graphic work it could be in this sort of uncertainty, where anticipation and monitoring are least under control, that sequential pattern can play an especially important part. This suggestion certainly makes good intuitive sense: old habits are likely to be a special hazard in time of overload or uncertainty.

ERRORS AS A FEATURE OF GROWTH

We generally think of errors as something we 'grow out of'. They may equally well be things we 'grow into', signs in fact that we have mastered a new way of going about some activity. In graphic work, children acquire a consistent way of working and they extend this pattern even to cases where it leads them astray. What they need to acquire is an awareness of those irregular occasions where the usual rules do not apply and a capacity to keep a watch over where their paths are leading.

This aspect of behaviour is in no way unique to graphic work. We have all heard children produce words such as 'foots', 'mouses', 'doed', 'goed', or 'costed'. These plurals and past tenses are not usually heard by children so they do not stem from imitation. Moreover, they often occur *after* a period when the child has used the irregular form correctly. What has happened is that the child has discovered a rule or pattern and is happily extending it to all nouns and verbs. Susan Ervin-Tripp and Wick Miller describe this behaviour as 'regularizing'. It needs to be followed by an awareness that some words do not follow the rule.

Behaviour of this kind has a significance beyond either graphic work or language. Remember that we use specific activities as vehicles for trying out general ideas about the nature of learning or the nature of people. In the present case, 'regularizing' behaviour inclines us towards the view that children's learning may be less the result of direct imitation than of abstracting and extending general patterns or 'rules' – of actively participating in their own early learning.

In addition, such behaviour alerts us to the possibility that each new mastery may bring its own problems, its own excess or own hazards. In a way, growing is continuous: success carries the continual risk of leading to a static style, and mastery is never complete.

5 Developing conventional equivalents

One aspect of working with shapes has to do with the way we learn that one thing (one shape) can stand for something else, that the two can mean the same thing. Learning equivalence in this way is a constant part of our lives, occurring each time we learn to apply with precision the terms 'same' and 'different'. Because of this, exploring questions of equivalence with shapes may both help us to learn about shapes and throw some light on general aspects of learning.

Consider first some of the more obvious equivalents we come to use in drawing. The shape of a mouth-line (up, down, or straight) stands for various feelings. The position of pupils in the eyes (centre, side, or top) stands for the direction of gaze. The bottom part of a page stands for the ground, the top for the sky. (But placing an object closer to the top may also mean that it is further away.) Hair flying stands for wind or for running. The frame of a comic-strip nearest the left of a page is 'the first', coming 'before' the others and marking the beginning of a story. A short check on comic-strips and book illustrations will yield many more equivalents of this kind, and it will also yield a sense of surprise that so many equivalents exist for feeling, position, time, sound, movement, collision, intention, and so on, even in work intended to be easily interpreted by children. Some of these equivalents have some relationship to the real world: hair does fly in a strong wind.

Others, however, have at best the status of a metaphor and one wonders how children ever come to decipher them (43). In fact, we have found, children often cannot decode many of the equivalents adults use and even adults may disagree unless the context or the whole story is given. In (43d), for example, is the plant moving up or down?

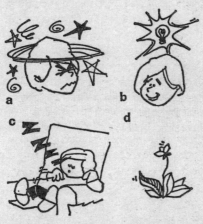

(43) Some conventional equivalents that children find hard to interpret. So of course can adults – is the plant in (d) moving up or down?

The way we perceive pictures is a research area of its own, an area recently highlighted by results like those reported by Barbara Lloyd, that show that people in cultures other than our own often do not see in 'our' pictures what is so obvious to us.[1] Results like these make clear the ambiguity in many drawings – the fact that there is usually more than one way of drawing an object and more than one way of interpreting a shape. Eyes, for instance, may be indicated by dots, straight lines, circles, triangles, shadings. And circles may be interpreted as balls, melons, heads, or holes.

How can we focus more directly on the production side of

equivalents, on the indicators we place in our own drawings rather than the indicators we can interpret? As with foreign languages, we can often understand more than we can produce; and the development of the two skills need not follow the same course or reflect the same conditions.

One way is to look directly at the equivalents that are produced for specific features of objects, detailing, for instance, the ages at which children make changes in the equivalents they use for light, shadows, depth, movement, time, feeling and so on. We might, for example, study the ages at which children indicate depth by placing one object above or behind another, by a change in the usual size of the distant object, or by foreshortening a near object. And we might, in a separate study, explore the ages at which they use different ways of signalling the sex of a person – clothing, for instance, or hair. A different way is to look for aspects that cut across a variety of features, asking: what general aspects are there to the ways we produce equivalents? what are the general ways in which equivalents differ from one another? Questions like these may lead us from the way children draw maps to the way they indicate time or movement, as we search constantly for some aspects that promise to cut across separate content areas. In this chapter and the next, four aspects are considered:

(1) *Coming to know what should be included.* Any equivalent naturally includes only some of the features of an original, just as any judgement about 'same' or 'different' involves paying attention to some features and ignoring others. In addition, these features must be related to one another in a way that can be counted as equivalent: otherwise the result may be like a shopping list, with pieces strung together as we happened to think of them. One of the first aspects of developmental change and individual difference, then, may be a shift in what children include and how the included parts are related to one another.

(2) *Learning the orthodox equivalent.* Any object or event can

recognizably be drawn in several ways, but among them some come to be used more often than others, come to be 'standard' equivalents. Can we observe children learning which these are? Can we discover some of the factors involved?

(3) *Agreeing on a point of view.* One of the conventions we often work with is that objects are drawn from a single point of view, usually as if we were gazing directly at the scene. Most drawings will also contain only what is visible, and because of this convention 'X-ray' drawings seem odd to us. How easily can children change a point of view? What is involved in adopting a different perspective?

(4) *Modifying old equivalents.* Students of children's art recognize that new equivalents often stem from modifying old ones: the first animals, for example, are usually humans with larger ears, or else humans turned sideways. In a sense, children proceed by themes or formulas with variations. What we are short of, however, is information about probable and improbable modifications, about changes that are likely and unlikely to occur given a type of drawing as starting point, and about the nature of resistance to change.

The first three aspects are explored in the remainder of this chapter; the fourth is covered in chapter 6.

LEARNING WHAT SHOULD BE INCLUDED

The essential point here is the *ambiguity* of what should be included. In the history of art, opinions about omissions and inclusions form a large part of discussions about the difference between various forms: 'art' *versus* 'caricature'; 'realist' or 'abstract' *versus* 'super-realist' equivalents for an original. Both Rudolf Arnheim and Ernst Gombrich underline the fact that ideas about appropriate omissions change from time to time and from culture to culture.[2]

Ambiguity also faces, however, the contemporary child

asked to produce an equivalent. We all know that 'pictures' may vary. We might expect, however, that a 'scientific' equivalent – such as a map – should be a fairly straightforward request. Take the case, for instance, of ten-year-olds in the United States asked to draw a map of the Mississippi river system. They were presented, 'to help you remember', with a map of the United States containing rivers and other geographical features. How much of this were they expected to put in? The request was part of a regular lesson in geography rather than an experiment. But the results illustrate the variety of interpretations the pupils can give to the request (44). Some drew a few rivers, some included many. Some drew only the part of the USA into which the Mississippi flows (the Gulf of Mexico); some sketched in the Eastern part of the United States while others showed more complete settings for the river system, either indicating the way the rivers were related to borders between states or the position of the rivers in the country as a whole.

Who is to decide which is the best interpretation of the term 'a map'? How do pupils come to know what should be included? What do they include?

Maps appear to be an ideal vehicle for exploring inclusions and omissions. Suppose, for instance, that we ask a younger group of children to copy a map that contains a variety of features, features that involve questions not only about what to include, but where to place it. Roslyn Dawes and I made a brief study of this kind with a map labelled 'the Australian Environment'. Within the outline of Australia are shown the usual lines dividing states, together with the names of different areas and some coloured markings indicating various geographical areas. Along the sides are frames showing various Australian animals and birds, together with the type of area where they normally occur (grasslands, forests, and so on).

Given such a map to copy, which features will children include and where will they place them?

A variety of solutions adopted by a group of Australian six-

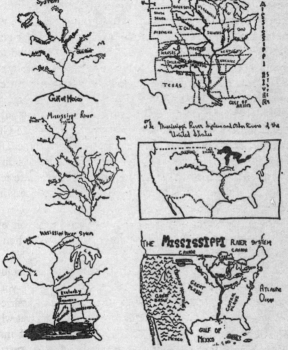

(44) Different responses to the request to 'draw the Mississippi River System' – copied from a map of the USA.

or seven-year-olds is shown in (45). The animals and birds were salient features for many of them; in some cases, the wild life was appropriately placed. In many others, it moved from the frame to within the outline, sometimes retaining Australian fauna, and sometimes metamorphosing into the children's own choices (like houses, or people). The maps in (45) also bring out a point that will crop up with several tasks: that knowledge about the usual inclusions and relationships does not necessarily go hand-in-hand with the ability to produce a

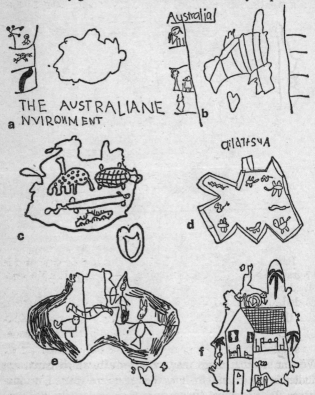

(45) Including and placing features in a map. Maps (a) and (b) are closest to the original in concept (position of animals in frame). Maps (c) to (f) shift the pictures to within the outline, and give some free versions of the pictures to be included. Concepts about position do not necessarily match skill in drawing and outline (compare (a) and (e)).

'good' shape (see 45a and e). The concept and the executive skill are different aspects of development.

Among the less 'decorative' features included, state lines were a prominent selection. Where towns and names were

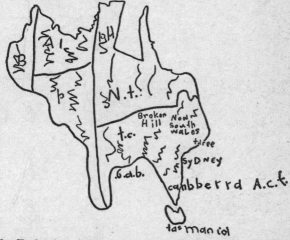

46) Early chauvinism: New South Wales is the home of this first-grade cartographer, who enlarges it and awards it the only marked cities.

included, they tended to be marked most often for the state in which the children lived (New South Wales). One such case is 46), an early version of chauvinism in mapping, with the home state swallowing two others and given the only marked cities.

We can see that maps may vary both in which parts are included in them and in how the parts are related to one another. Relationships among parts seem especially likely to reveal differences between individuals and between ages. Suppose then we set a task where the relationship is the major part of the request. We shall ask Australian children ranging from five to eleven to 'draw a map of the way you go from home to school'.

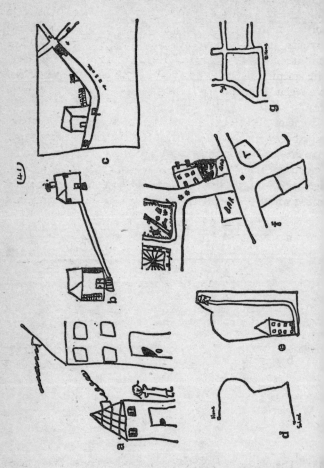

(47) Acquiring the conventions of a map: varying solutions to the problem 'draw a map of the way from home to school' cover: juxtaposition only, a single connecting line, and various indications of direction, distance and setting.

What we find first of all is that children often present us with 'pictures'. We are accustomed to the idea that 'olde worlde' maps frequently contain prominent pictures of sea-serpents, monsters, dragons, and so forth. But the current convention is for a distinction between 'maps' and 'pictures', with 'pictures' appearing only as a small extra, carefully tied to a legend that shows the tourist what to expect in a given area.

Some of the children's pictures contain no sign of relation-ships between parts, other than that objects are next to one another – child, home, and school arranged in a row, with no connecting route (47*a*). Others begin to include a road, together with indications of direction, distance, and general setting within a network of roads (47*b – g*). By and large, the

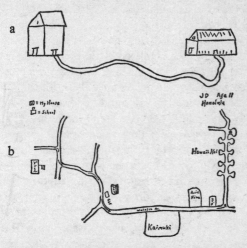

48) The effects of experience with conventions. These maps were intended to 'show the way from home to school'; (*a*) is by a fifteen-year-old Limbu boy, whose home and school were not in fact on the same path; (*b*) is by a cartographically more practised eleven-year-old American.

older the child, the more likely he or she is to include direction and general setting (distance is seldom marked), and to omit pictures. This progression does not always hold, however; some older children continue to produce pictures without relationships, while a few young children produce adult-type equivalents, suggesting that interest and experience are important factors. This would fit with Frances Dart's and La Panna Pradhan's finding that Nepalese children, with little experience in reading or writing maps, draw 'pictorial' maps at an age when most US children are using adult conventions. The difference is clearly revealed in (48).

What possibilities, other than road-lines, could be used for showing relationships? One important way could be called '*living geography*', that is, the map is organized in terms of what is important to us as individuals. This may mean giving a prominent or central position to our own landmarks. Or, especially with children, it may mean indicating one's own actions in a map, with parts related by the order in which these actions are carried out. Two striking examples are presented in (49): they are almost step-by-step walks with the ups and downs of the path very much in mind. They may not be what we typically call 'maps' but they are of more interest to an environmental psychologist than conventional productions.

Actions as features to be included and as ways of relating features constantly recur in children's equivalents, as we shall see when we come to discuss equivalents for rhythm. But they are not as exclusive to children as we might at first think. Many of us, for example, generate lists of things to be done – shopping lists, work lists – by a mental walk through an area or a day. And all of us are familiar with the difference between moving through an area as a driver and moving through it as a passenger. To be a passenger may mean acquiring no knowledge of how to get from A to B the next time round.

Such 'cognitive mapping' seems dependent on the intention

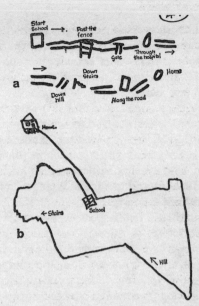

49) Living geography: the parts included, and their order, reflect significant actions rather than objective distance or direction (a) is by a girl, (b) by a boy, both aged eight.

remember and on having actively participated in the process of passing through.

LEARNING THE ORTHODOX EQUIVALENT

Most objects or events can be recognizably depicted by more than one equivalent. We can, for instance, recognize movement by the way arms or legs are placed, by the lean of the body, or the streaming of hair and clothing. In addition, we know that some equivalents are more orthodox than others, and that equivalents do change from time to time. This change seems especially likely when the original has no visual shape. Musical

notation, for instance, has changed a great deal over the cen
turies, reflecting a shift from a polynomial system, where eac
symbol stands for a sequence of notes sharing some relation
ship, to a monomial system, where in general each symbo
stands just for one sound.

Suppose we concentrate on occasions where the origina
has no visual form. What do children do, for instance, whe
asked to write the equivalent of a piece of music, or a series c
sounds tapped out on a table? We know a certain amoun
about this as a result of Jeanne Bamberger's investigation c
particular features of children's understanding of music a
opposed to adults'.[4] Bamberger felt that children were ofte
handicapped in their listening to music by not having playe
an active organizing role in listening – they needed, she though
to find their own 'groupings, cohesions, centres of focus
With this end in view, she asked children in elementar
school to 'draw a picture of the piece showing just wha
happened', showing how and where the music sometime
changed into 'something different'. The drawings showed
number of the variations we would expect from the othe
'maps'. That is, some children drew pictures with no relation
ships indicated. Some drew chains of items with no specif
ordering or grouping. And some drew groups of items with th
grouping related to events in the piece played for then

Jeanne Bamberger also observed that the features ofte
marked in the children's notations were not always the sam
as those marked in standard musical notation. The end no
in a group of notes, for example, was often drawn different
from others in the group, marking, as it were, the end of
functional part, or the 'arrival at a goal'.

Some further data is provided by Miriam Stambak's askir
children to tap out the sound equivalent of a set of dots, wit
(..); (. .); (.. ..); or (.. .. ...).[5] At age six, she found, only 2 p
cent understood at the outset that the interval in (..) should

shorter than the interval in (. .). By age eight, 54 per cent understood, and by age twelve, 96 per cent. In addition, she found a difference between understanding the symbol (visual space for auditory space) and being able to give an accurate translation of longer messages. Once again, the concept (knowledge of the equivalent) and the executive skill (translation into action) were shown to be far from identical.

Suppose we were to turn Stambak's task around and ask children to write out for us a series they had heard. To keep the number of possibilities down to a manageable level, we should specify that for each tap they could use a dot and that the message should be written from left to right on the page. When I tried this in 1971, I found the youngest children often showed no equivalent for an interval; they wrote down the given number of circles, or just wrote 'many' circles.[6] One of the first equivalents to emerge was an 'action' equivalent, similar in many ways to the 'living geography' of (49). The children would write down dots for the first grouping, pause, then write further dots for the second group, yielding a series without any spatial gap (examples 1 and 2 in 50a).

(50) Translating a series of maps into visual form; the versions in (a) are by five-to-seven-year-olds, those in (b) by a nine-year-old.

In the same figure, example 3 shows the use of a standard spatial gap, with no other difference between the two groups. Example 4 shows size used as an equivalent, yielding a 'hen-and-chickens' picture that certainly does look in a way like 1-3 grouping. Examples 5 and 6 illustrate the use of position on the page combined with a spatial gap: two equivalents for the one auditory interval.

To our eyes, the use of *two* equivalents – position and gap, or size and gap – may seem excessive, to be a 'flourish' that the translation does not call for. By age six or so, certainly the 'flourishes' had dropped out, and the majority of children were using the conventional single equivalent.

Clearly we are dealing with some form of learning, probably some aspect of a 'hidden curriculum' rather than a result of direct teaching. Coming to use the orthodox equivalent, however, may not be the whole story. Children are aware that more than one equivalent is possible. They make a choice among a number of 'possibles', a point made clear by a nine-year-old who responded to my 'why' questions by saying: 'I can do it other ways'(50b). His learning, then, was not limited to one orthodox equivalent, but also covered a range of possibilities.

This sense of 'the possible' seems also to be an aspect of learning beyond children of seven. Take, for instance, the three sets of answers shown in (51): records for three children, all asked to write out as many equivalents as possible. The first child (age nine) ended with the statement: 'I could put anything here!' On this assertion, she declined to go beyond the eight equivalents she had generated. The second child (age eleven) was asked if you could 'put anything there, for instance an X'. He rejected the 'X' on the grounds that it already had a meaning, namely multiplication. The third child – age twelve, but thought to have learning problems, especially in reading – produced first an action equivalent, then two combinations of size and gap. She would venture no opinion about whether you could 'put anything there' or not.

(51) More translations of maps into visual form; (a) by a nine-year-old, (b) by an eleven-year-old, (c) by a twelve-year-old but with 'learning problems'.

Looking at these children suggests that one slowly evolving aspect of their learning may follow a path similar to that found in the history of musical notation, namely a shift from using two equivalents for one interval towards a more standard one-for-one relationship. Learning an orthodox form may carry with it a great deal of learning about what is best, what is possible, and what is absolutely out of court. In effect, learning and using a standard visual form may not be so different from learning and using other appropriate forms of behaviour, from ways of talking to table manners.

AGREEING ON A POINT OF VIEW

Several parts of the same drawing may be linked up to one another by connecting lines or by connecting actions. In addition, they may be related by the fact that they are all drawn from a particular point of view. The usual convention in our culture is that we draw all parts as they would appear if seen straight-on with the head stationary. As a result, we find rather strange 'Egyptian' pictures where the eye is drawn as seen from the front though the rest of the figure is 'side-on', or drawings by Picasso that combine in one face features seen from several points of view.

Not all cultures agree that equivalents should show things as they look rather than as they are. And not all cultures agree that the appropriate point of view, even for things as-they-look, is straight-on. In many Chinese paintings, for instance, it is accepted that drawing is done as if from a small rise above the scene.

A great deal has already been written about the development of a single point of view, the use of perspective, and the general conviction that things should be drawn the way they look rather than the way they really are. For our purposes, the important thing to realize is that more than one point of view is possible. We also need to be aware that most people operate within the limits of what is common within a culture, and that acquiring the accepted point of view is part of the learning and inventing that children engage in.

We can observe some of this learning, inventing, and selecting when children draw humans 'side-on'. To find out what would happen in a case where earlier practice could have little or no effect, Roslyn Dawes and I asked children to 'draw your school the way it would look from the air'. For some children, the only change that occurs is in their own position: the school remains unchanged, or changes only in size (52). Other children show more awareness that the building must be drawn differently, either as if seen at a 45 degree oblique or, more commonly, as if seen from directly overhead. Once the view is overhead, a prominent feature must be the roof. In fact, many children draw the roof only (53b). The roof keeps

me of the pictorial features (like the tiles and chimney-pots
3c and d)), but eventually these drop out to yield a non-pic-
rial layout (e – g). By and large, this progression occurs as chil-
ren develop, but with some notable exceptions: for instance,
) and (g) by ten-year-olds, but (f) is from a boy of five.

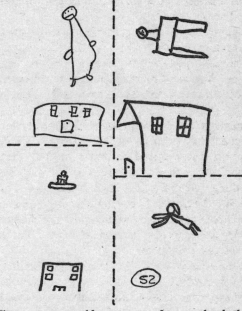

2) First attempts to 'draw a map of your school, the way it
oks from the air'. In these, the school changes only in size or
t at all; the position of the observer carries the meaning.

A view from the air is clearly a difficult problem for children.
'hy? First, you need to recognize that the world will have a
ifferent appearance. Next, you need to work out in what way
will be different. And finally, you need to work out a way of
nowing on paper what you know – a way that others will
ccept.

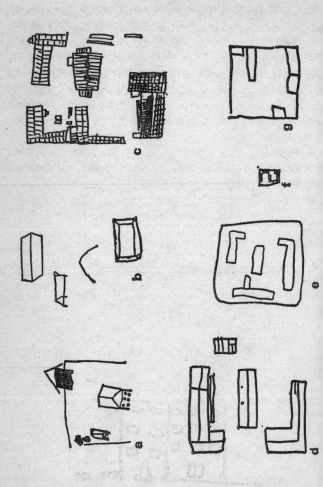

(53) Later drawings of school from the air. The roof comes
be emphasized and a diagram form, without pictorial detai
emerges.

The last step is of particular interest. Take, for example,
children who wish to indicate that from above you will be able
to see both the roof of the school and also two or more sides.
How are they to do this? And what gets in the way? Part of the
difficulty appears to be an early equivalent, namely the use of a
horizontal line as the ground. As long as this base – and only
this base – can stand for ground, then the only way to show both
roof and sides is to connect all lines to the one base or to open
up the sides of the building as if they were pages in a book (54).
Once the single equivalent is given up, then the way is open
for imaginative buildings (55a), or for front and side at the usual
acute angle to one another (55b).

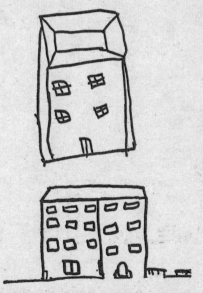

54) What happens when you use the horizontal to indicate the
ground, when you want to show more than one façade of school,
seen from the air'.

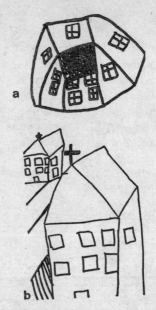

(55) Solutions made possible by using non-horizontal line to indicate the ground.

Why should it be difficult to part with an old equivalent? I may be that using new reference points requires a gener intellectual change. This is certainly the view of Jean Piag and Bärbel Inhelder. Younger children, they argue, tend use as a base, or as a reference point for a unit, some other un that happens to be close by. For this reason, they progres along a series of steps, A to B, B to C, C to D, rather than b way of an overall grasp. In pictures, this phenomenon appear with special clarity in the relationship of chimneys to roofs o houses to roads (56). The base line taken is the line immediatel adjacent rather than any more distant point that requires som mental bridging of space.

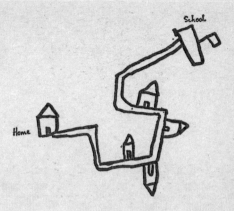

(56) Ground-lines and reference points: what alternative relationships between road and houses are feasible?

Another reason is likely to be the awkwardness or ease of any alternative to the old equivalent. In (56), for instance, there is no easy place to put the houses 'on the other side of the road'. In similar fashion, once we abandon the security of a single line that always stands for the ground, then any position on the paper has many possible meanings. It may stand for higher ground (as in a hill), for something higher in the air (as in the top of a building), for ground that is farther away from the viewer, or for something that is both farther away and higher. Given such ambiguity, we might all be reluctant to leave a clear-cut notation.

Both these reasons draw our attention to the fact that, when it comes to learning or inventing equivalents, there is no question of a 'blank slate'. As in all problem-solving, we start from something we already do, rather than from a neutral state, and that something may either help or hinder us. The nature of help and hindrance, and the way modifications occur with old equivalents, are the topics of the next chapter.

6 From old to new equivalents

In the course of time, children come to expand the range of objects they can draw, and they draw old objects in new ways. How do new equivalents come into their repertoires? Among young children, only the verbal label may be altered. The one scribble may be labelled 'Mummy' or 'a train'. Once children do begin to offer different drawings for different objects, however, how do the differences come about?

The starting point is often a 'formula' of some kind. All children tend to repeat a particular way of working, both for simple and for complex drawings (57). These formulas are then often changed in small ways: the themes acquire small variations. We may see, for example, variations in size among the formula figures used for families, not always in correspondence with the actual sizes of the people drawn (58). Or we may see human shapes modified slightly to create animals. The animal in (59), for instance, is a formula human turned sideways and given two additional legs. And all the shapes in (60) are of animals, despite their human appearance. All four sets were drawn in response to a request for drawings of 'animals at the zoo', The first two (a and b) appear to us completely 'human'. The second two (c and d) introduce changes in head and legs for the elephant and the bull, but the gorilla is a standard human.

It has been recognized for a long time that drawings of

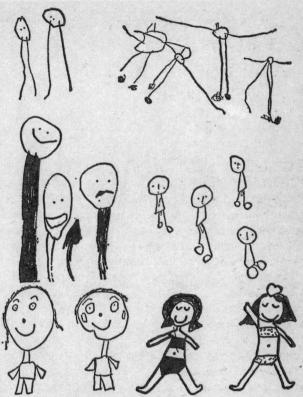

(57) 'Formula' drawings, simple and complex.

humans or animals are developed by small modifications. Maps too are also often constructed by modifying such familiar shapes as rectangles, circles, or ovals (61).

But little is known about the way these modifications take place. Which part of a figure is modified most readily and which parts are the last to be changed? What kinds of modification are most likely with different kinds of figures? Do some figures invite one kind of modification but resist another?

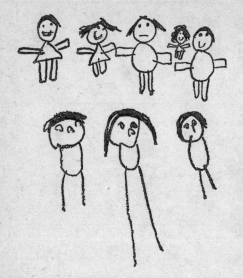

(58) 'Formula' drawings for families, with variations in size.

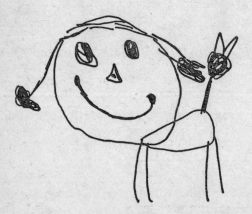

(59) Lady into cat; modification of a human formula.

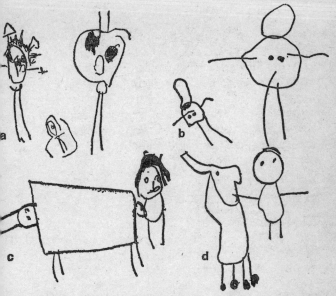

(60) Animals at the zoo: variations on a standard core (*a*) koala,
monkey and tiger, (*b*) lizard in hat, tiger in hat, (*c*) bull and
gorilla, (*d*) elephant and gorilla.

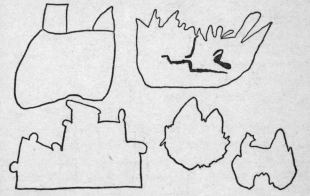

(61) Modifying basic shapes to produce a map of Australia.

Roslyn Dawes, Rochelle Levine and I have explored these questions in two ways. One is by collecting children's repeated drawings: asking them, at regular intervals, to draw us 'a person'. We can then examine their drawings for the types of change that occur. The other is by asking children for an equivalent we know they seldom use spontaneously. We chose movement, and asked children either to draw for us two people (one walking, one running), or else a single person bending over to pick up a ball.

REPEATED DRAWINGS

The classic accounts of development have been studies of single children extending over two or more years: G. H. Luquet's daughter, for example, or Helga Eng's niece.[1] If we want to look at a larger sample of children, we have to be content with shorter periods of time (because many children are certain to move or drop out of the study), aiming specially at those ages (for example, three to five years), where change is most likely, and at figures where it is reasonable to ask for a couple of tries over a short period of time (for instance, drawings of humans).

Two students working with me have collected such repeated drawings, over periods of two to six months. The first collection was made by Rochelle Levine, in a fairly well-to-do suburb in the USA. The other was made by Roslyn Dawes, in an inner-city area of Sydney where a majority of the parents were low-income, and frequently immigrants who were not English-speaking and were limited in their own schooling. This second sample turned out to be the better for our purposes. Changes were slower and easier to observe, largely we suspect, because the children did not draw as frequently either in nursery school or at home.

One of the first problems we came across was the difficulty

f saying for certain whether drawings were the 'same' as one nother, whether a change had occurred or not. There is unfortunately no available taxonomy, no accepted way of classifying humans. Roslyn Dawes and I finally settled for the following terms:

(a) No change, as illustrated by three of the four humans in the upper row of (62), and in the first pair of the lower row.

(b) A change in the position or number of 'accessories', such as a change from two stick-lines to four, a change in the position or length of the limbs, the addition of facial features, or the addition of ears. These changes are illustrated across most pairs of occasions in (63).

(c) A change in the way the core is constructed: that is, the number of solids used for the head, torso, and legs. Changes of this sort are illustrated in (63) (also compare the last two pairs in each series).

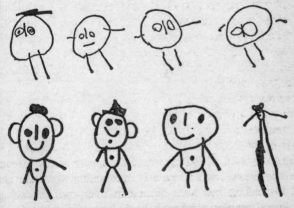

62) Repeated drawings over twelve weeks: only the accessories change here, not the manner of constructing the torso or core.

In all, we collected four drawings from each of 46 children, the 46 who were in their pre-schools on all of the occasions

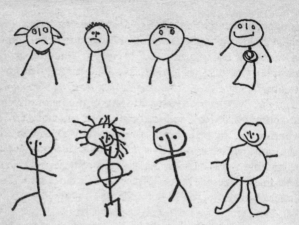

(63) Repeated drawings over twelve weeks: changes in the core occur in these drawings.

we visited. The first two visits were a week apart, the second and third three weeks apart, the third and fourth five week apart. For these 46 'regulars' we then analysed only change from one occasion to the next.

The result that struck us most was the small number o changes of the third kind. There could theoretically have bee 138 such changes, but in fact, there were less than 30. In effect most changes were not changes in the core but in the acces sories only; that left the main units and the main boundarie between units undisturbed. How then does major chang come about?

One route to change may in fact lie through playing wit the accessories. This possibility is certainly suggested b drawings where the legs are in a 'straddled' position (64 Given a human with two stick-lines extending down from single circle, an easy next step is to take a single line across between the legs. This gives the figure a very different appea ance: to our eyes, the appearance of a solid figure. An examp is the first two drawings in (64), drawn two weeks apart by the same child. This type of change may stem from an accidental discovery of solid figures in the course of filling in an empty centre, as in (64c). The transition, unfortunately, is not easy to observe over time. Our supposition is given some support, though, by the sequences children often use when constructing 'straddled' figures: a sequence in which the cross-line creating a solid core is added last (65a–d). This sequence is not at all invariable: for instance, the left leg was drawn first as a single line but the rest of the core was constructed as a solid, and in (f), the core triangle was drawn first, and the legs attached afterwards. In early drawings, however, the cross-line-last sequence does seem to predominate.

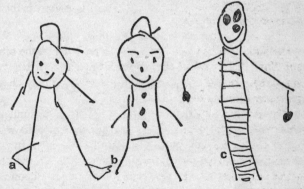

(64)   Possible development for figures with straddled legs; (a) and (b) are drawings two weeks apart by the same child, with the cross-bar added last; (c) shows the sort of decoration that could suggest that adding a cross-bar makes a figure 'solid'.

REQUESTING MOVEMENT

If we want to observe change, we can either wait for it to occur, (in which case we are very likely to see changes in the accessories and very unlikely to see them in the core). Or alter-

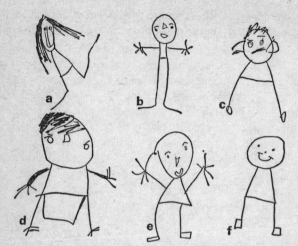

(65) Drawing sequences for figures with straddled legs; (a–d) the cross-bar is added last; (e) part of the torso is drawn as a unit; in (f) the complete torso is drawn as a unit.

natively, we can encourage change by asking for equivalents that children do not often produce spontaneously, for features that are not often included in children's drawings. The feature Roslyn Dawes and I chose was movement. We wanted to know which parts of the body were most likely to be modified, and which parts would be the last to be changed.

FIRST STUDY: WALKING AND RUNNING

We asked children between five and ten years old to draw us two people: one a person walking slowly, the other a person running fast. We found the children's most frequent equivalent for a change of speed was a change in the legs. They might simply draw them further apart, or they might change the angle of feet and legs (66). This type of change presents an awkward problem for children who usually draw their figures with legs far apart. These are, in a sense, left with no room for change since they have pre-empted the most available equivalent already (67).

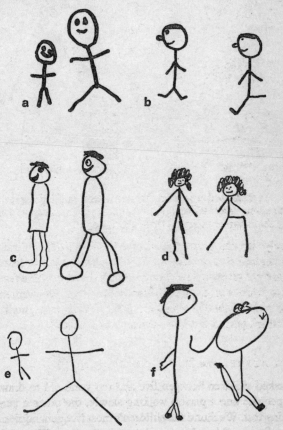

(66) Equivalents for movement. In each pair, drawn by the same child, one is walking slowly, the other running fast. In these examples, only one equivalent is used: a change in the position of the legs.

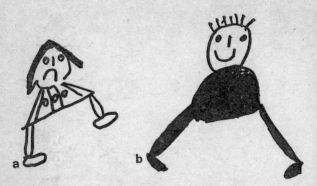

(67) A problem in developing an equivalent for running: the commonest – legs far apart – is already part of this child's standard figure. The walking figure (*a*) was drawn first.

The children also commonly changed arm position, but only when they also changed leg position (68*a* – *c*). Thirdly, they often 'streamed', either hair or clothing, or also indicated streaming by movement lines (69).

The last cue (last in terms of age) that they used was a change in the axis of the figure itself. In most earlier drawings, the arms and legs may change but the torso remains firmly upright. Changes in the torso itself were found almost exclusively among the nine- and ten-year-olds. Some examples are given in (69). Specially interesting is (69*a*), where the torso is no longer rigidly upright but the entire figure leans. There is no 'give' in the legs, and all parts of the torso stick firmly to single-axis principle.

As they get older then, we find children use more and more equivalents for movement, first altering the legs, and changing the upright torso last of all, really quite late in childhood. This initial preference for an upright torso, with all its parts on a single axis, fits in with what we know about the way children will often draw distorted or upside-down humans rather than

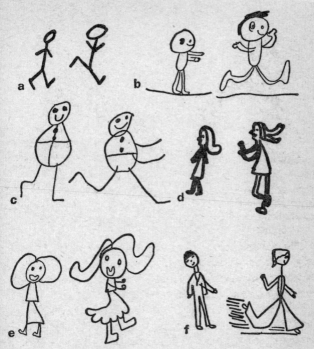

68) More equivalents for movement. These cover changes in legs and arms, 'streaming' of hair and clothes, and movement lines. But with one possible exception, the torso stays upright.

alter the single axis of the body. Faced with all these ramrod humans, we could not resist the temptation to ask for drawings where the posture had to be abandoned – drawings of a person bending over to pick up a ball.

SECOND STUDY: BENDING

What will children do when asked to draw a bending figure? The principle of all parts on a single axis seems so entrenched that we should expect a variety of solutions to this request,

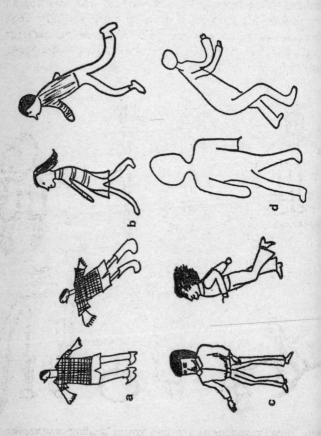

(69) Further equivalents for movement. These change the angle of the figure to the ground. All are by children aged nine to twelve years.

lutions that may be extremely creative but that still retain
e single axis.

One early solution is simply to place the two parts of the
roblem – the person and the ball – close together, but without
y relationship between them other than proximity (69).
ext, modifications may be made either in the ball (its
sition or the number of balls) or in one part of the figure,
mely the arm (70).

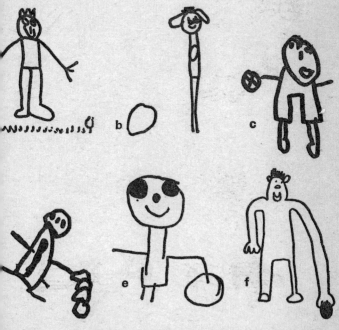

70)   Small variations on a theme: figures bending over to pick
p a ball. Solutions here cover juxtaposition without any change
the figure, changes in the position of the ball, and changes in
e arm of the figure.

When the body itself begins to change, we do indeed fi
that children stay with a single axis for the torso (71a). Th
may shift to a figure like an inverted V, or an inverted
(71b to e), but even with these the legs still form a single ax
with no sign of a bend at the knees. Only later do the le
themselves shift from being so stiffly upright, so that we beg
to see figures that contain four or more lines of directic
within the body (71f – i).

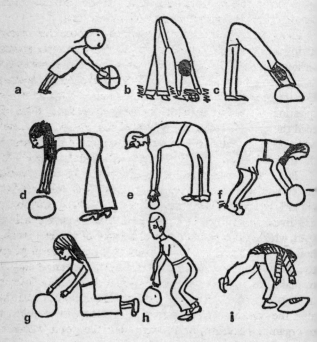

(71) Larger variations on the theme of picking up a ball. The
include various ways of modifying the usual upright, single-ax
figure.

ASPECTS OF CHANGE

Our two studies, running and bending, both illustrate ways in which we can explore openness and resistance to change. By and large, we find that children make changes most easily where they may simply add on an extra item, without giving up any general principle such as the principle of not invading space belonging to some other item, or the principle of arranging parts in a given order or on a given axis.

The more difficult changes appear to be those that involve giving up a principle that normally governs the way we arrange various items. The difference between these fundamental changes and the easier ones is not only to be found in drawings. For instance, in learning to ask questions – such as 'when' questions – the first transition is likely to be from 'John will read the book' to 'John will read the book when?': the simple addition of an extra item. Later changes move the 'when' to the front of the phrase – 'When John will read the book?' – but the last change is one that breaks up the initial order, splitting the two parts of the verb to yield: 'When will John read the book?'[2] This sort of resistance is familiar also in our own everyday lives: in any problem where we need to change a basic plan, whether this plan concerns the layout of a week's work, a holiday, a journey, or the logistics of getting several people to different points at much the same time, the easiest changes to make are those at the fringe – small changes, for instance in days or times. The more difficult changes are those that alter the core of a layout: decisions to delete, to combine, to re-organize priorities, or to start from the point where we expected to end.

7 Last words

My hope is that you have now acquired some new ways of looking at children's graphic work, whether the product is a letter of the alphabet, a 'picture', or a map. This section is intended as a brief and incomplete answer to the questions: What can we now say about the way children draw? What can we look for and think about?

One recurring theme has been the usefulness of looking at any piece of graphic work as a set of parts or units combined into a whole or pattern. This leads us to some fairly direct questions, such as: What are the parts like? How are they related to one another and to the whole? With these questions, the following features emerge from children's work:

(1) *Children are thrifty in their use of units.* That is, they will use one graphic unit (a particular kind of circle, a particular 'sun-shape', a particular type of human figure) over and over. The same line, for instance, often doubles as an arm or a leg; the same human figure stands for every member of the family. If you wish to look back at some examples, see (1), (8), (57) and (58). In all of these, the repetition of units helps create a sense of charming simplicity or unity. It also serves as a reminder to us that the child is developing not just a type of line but also a concept, discovering similarities and realizing that many separate items may be represented by a single symbol.

(2) *When children do make a change, they are usually con-*

rvative. Typically, a change in meaning will be carried, specially among younger children, by varying only one unit ometimes only by varying the name given to the drawing). The family members in (72a), for instance, vary only in height nd in the type of smile. Which parts are most likely to be aried? What we have found is that variation occurs mainly in ome 'accessory' parts of a drawing, leaving the 'core' un-isturbed. Humans reach for an object, for instance, by

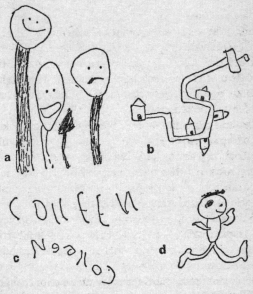

72) A variety of intriguing features of children's art are uried in this collection.

xtending only their arms, the rest of the body remaining lissfully upright (70). And humans also often run simply by a hange in the distance between the two legs (66).

The human in (72d) is an 'advanced' and less conservative

drawing than usual. The child has indicated movement b
extending both legs and arms, by turning the body side-o
and by giving a realistic flip to each foot. Note also that th
drawing does not display a very common form of thrift: that i
the two arms and the two legs are not drawn in identic
fashion. The legs are not like the arms and (even more impo
tant) each foot is not like the other, each arm is not at exactl
the same angle. The core of the body, nonetheless (the hea
and torso) remains staunchly upright. You will, in fac
rarely see an intentional departure from a 90 degree uprigh
in a child's drawing and, when it occurs, that child will ofte
be noted as 'talented'.

We are led to wonder: Why are such changes so difficult t
make? Part of the answer lies in children discovering tha
unwary change often leads them into unexpected difficulties
'a problem solved is a problem created'. Part of the answer als
lies in a third feature to drawings: the way parts are related t
one another.

(3) *Parts are related to one another according to specifi
principles.* Some of these principles refer to the way each uni
may be allotted its 'own space', its own boundaries. Loo
again, for instance, at the running figure (72*d*). For all th
elegant treatment of limbs, most parts of the body are con
tained in their own spaces, neatly marked off from any othe
The legs are the exception: a single flowing line combines le
and foot and unites both legs with a single contour. If you wis
to look back at some other examples of spaces and boundarie
and at the efforts children will go to avoid having parts overla
– one part crossing the boundary or violating the space o
another part – look back to chapter 2, especially (14) and (15
and the section on how children solve the problem of addin
extra wheels to a train (23).

Some other linking principles have to do with orientatio
Children prefer to have the main parts of the body arrange

along a single axis, almost as if the parts were strung along a straight piece of wire. Children also prefer as a rule, once they have discovered that the horizontal stands for the ground, to place figures at a firm 90 degrees to the ground. (You will have often noticed, also, that the arms are usually at 90 degrees to the body). These preferred axes or reference systems apply not only to the way humans are drawn. Look, for instance, at the houses in (72b). The sketch is one child's version of the way home from school. Part of the overall effect stems from the principle 'each to its own space': the houses do not overlap one another, or cross the lines of the street. In addition, however, each house stands at a neat 90 degrees to its ground-line. If the houses had chimneys, they would undoubtedly also be drawn at a neat 90 degrees to their immediate reference line, the roof.

Uncovering the principles that link parts of any graphic work helps us be more observant. We become less inclined to regard children's efforts as 'odd', and more ready to see that their 'errors' are often the result of the careful application of some of the rules they use. Their rules may not be ours, but they are nonetheless rules rather than exercises in pure whimsy.

(4) *Parts are related to one another in a sequence.* Next time you watch a child draw, note where the drawing starts and ends, and ask yourself: How would I describe this sequence? How is it likely to change with practice or with age? What follows from the sequence? Do certain sequences, for example, lead to particular types of end-result?

The nature and effects of sequence are the burden of chapters 3 and 4, with consequences ranging from omitted parts to upside-down humans. At this point, let me offer simply one reminder of an effect, in the form of the names written in (72c). The top name was written from left to right; the bottom name (a 'reversal') was written from right to left. You might try for yourself printing your name from right to left – quickly and without too much deliberation – and note how the starting point and the direction of work influence the end-result. In effect, each step we take in any graphic work has consequences for later steps. Our task is to unravel the consequences and the way these are coped with.

(5) *Children's graphic work illustrates their thinking and ours.* It is tempting to separate areas of experience from one another allotting each to its 'own space': 'drawing' separate from 'thinking'; 'the eye' separate from 'the mind'; the 'arts' from the 'sciences'; the 'soft' sciences from the 'hard'. One may easily end by feeling that an interest in graphic work is not completely academically respectable: learning to read words or to count is surely a more important area, a critical skill rather than a 'frill'. And children's drawings of people may seem especially suspect. How can such sources of pleasure be part of 'science'?

I have tried to convince you that you should feel no guilt. Graphic work is truly 'visible thinking'. The features it displays – thrift, conservatism, principles of organization and sequence – are features of all problem-solving, whether by children or adults. If you begin to note these features in one area of experience – children's graphic work – then you may begin to note them in your own thinking and problem-solving. In effect, I hope you may begin to see children's graphic work not only as 'visible thinking' but even as a 'slice of life'.

References

1. WHY STUDY CHILDREN'S DRAWINGS? (pp. 9-30)

1. R. Arnheim, *Visual Thinking* (Berkeley, Calif.: University of California Press, 1969).
2. K. J. Connolly and J. S. Bruner (eds), *The Growth of Competence* (New York and London: Academic Press, 1974).
3. J. Piaget and B. Inhelder, *The Psychology of the Child* (London: Routledge, 1969).
4. K. J. Connolly and J. S. Bruner (eds), *The Growth of Competence*.
5. J. Flavell, 'Developmental studies of mediated memory', in H. W. Reese and L. P. Lipsitt (eds), *Advances in Child Development and Behaviour*, 5 (New York and London: Academic Press, 1970).
6. N. Bernstein, *The Coordination and Regulation of Movement* (Oxford: Pergamon Press, 1967).
7. G. A. Miller, E. Galanter and K. Pribram, *Plans and the Structure of Action* (New York and London: Holt, Rinehart & Winston, 1960).
8. R. Arnheim, *Visual Thinking*.
9. R. Kellogg, *Analyzing Children's Art* (Palo Alto, Calif.: National Press, 1969).
10. D. Booth, 'Pattern-painting by the young child: a cognitive developmental approach', MEd thesis, University of Sydney, 1974.
11. J. Piaget and B. Inhelder, *The Child's Conception of Space* (London: Routledge, 1956).
12. K. S. Lashley, 'The problem of serial order in behaviour', in L. A. Jeffress (ed), *Cerebral Mechanisms in Behaviour: the Hixon Symposium* (New York: Wiley, 1951).
13. M. L. J. Abercrombie, R. L. Lindon and M. C. Tyson, 'Direction of drawing movements', *Developmental Medicine and Child Neurology*, 1968, *10*, 83-97.

14. D. R. Olson, *Cognitive Development: the Child's Acquisition of Diagonality* (New York and London: Academic Press, 1970).
15. A. Marshack, *The Roots of Civilization* (New York: McGraw Hill 1972). A. Marshack, 'Upper paleolithic notation and symbol' *Science*, 1972, *178*, 817-28.
16. E. H. Gombrich, *Art and Illusion* (London: Phaidon, 1960).

2. DRAWINGS AS PATTERNS (pp. 31-58)

1. D. A. Dondis, *A Primer of Visual Literacy* (Cambridge, Mass. MIT Press, 1973).
2. R. Arnheim, *Art and Visual Perception* (Berkeley, Calif.: University of California Press, 1954).
3. R. Arnheim, *Visual Thinking*, p. 251.
4. R. Kellogg, *Analyzing Children's Art*.
5. R. Kellogg, *Analyzing Children's Art*, p. 61.
6. R. Kellogg, *Analyzing Children's Art*, p. 176.
7. D. Booth, 'Pattern-painting by the young child'.
8. T. Munro, 'Children's art abilities: studies at the Cleveland Museum of Art', in E. W. Eisner and D. W. Ecker (eds), *Readings in Art Education* (London: Ginn-Blaisdell, 1966) p. 173.
9. R. Kellogg, *Analyzing Children's Art*.
10. R. Kellogg, *Analyzing Children's Art*, p. 160.
11. N. H. Freeman, 'Process and product in children's drawing' *Perception*, 1972, *1*, 123-40.
12. H. S. M. Coxeter, 'The mathematical implications of Escher's prints', in J. L. Locher (ed), *The World of N. C. Escher* (New York: Abrams, 1971).
13. K. Lewin, *A Dynamic Theory of Personality* (New York: McGraw-Hill, 1935).

3. SEQUENCE IN CHILDREN'S DRAWINGS (pp. 59-81)

1. L. Ghent, 'Form and its orientation: a child's eye view', *American Journal of Psychology*, 1961, *74*, 177-90.
2. H. Eng, *The Psychology of Children's Drawings* (London: Kegan Paul, 1931).
3. M. Bernbaum, 'Accuracy in children's copying: the role of different stroke sequences and school experience', PhD dissertation, George Washington University, 1974.
4. B. S. Mann and E. B. Lehman, 'Transparencies in children's human figure drawings: a developmental approach', *Studies in Art Education*, 1976 (in press).

5. K. Inuma and K. Watanabe, 'Observations on moving objects drawn by children: orientation and motion of railway trains', *Japanese Journal of Psychology*, 1937, *12*, 393-408 (*Psychological Abstracts*, 1938, *12*, 109, No 997).
6. J. J. Goodnow and S. Friedman, 'Orientations in Children's human figure drawings: an aspect of graphic language', *Developmental Psychology*, 1972, 7, 10-16.
7. F. L. Ilg and L. B. Ames, *School Readiness* (New York: Harper & Row, 1964)
8 N. H. Freeman, 'Do children draw men with arms coming out of the head?' *Nature*, 1975, *254*, 416-7.

4. COPYING SIMPLE SHAPES (pp. 82-111)

1. A. Gesell and L. B. Ames, 'The development of directionality in drawing', *Journal of Genetic Psychology*, 1946, *68*, 45-61.
2. F. L. Ilg and L. B. Ames, *School Readiness*.
3. J. J. Goodnow and R. Levine, 'The grammar of action: sequence and syntax in children's copying of simple shapes', *Cognitive Psychology*, 1973, *4*, 82-98.
4. M. Bernbaum, 'Accuracy in children's copying'.
5. M. Bernbaum, 'Accuracy in children's copying', p. 79.
6. D. Diringer, *The Alphabet* (London: Hutchinson, 1968).
7. C. Donoghue, *The Development of Writing*, Jackdaw No 47 (New York: Grossman, undated).
8. J. J. Goodnow, S. Friedman, M. Bernbaum and E. B. Lehman, 'Direction and sequence in copying'.
9. A. Lieblich and A. Ninio, 'Developmental trends in directionality of drawing in Jewish and Arab Israeli children', *Journal of Cross-Cultural Psychology*, 1976 (in press).
10. A. Lieblich and A. Ninio, 'Developmental trends in directionality'.
11. W. Dennis and E. Raskin, 'Further evidence concerning the effect of handwriting habits on the location of drawings', *Journal of Consulting Psychology*, 1960, *24*, 548-49.
12. L. G. Braine, 'Asymmetries of pattern perception observed in Israelis'. *Neuropsychologia*, 1968, *6*, 73-88.
13. A. Gesell and L. B. Ames, 'The development of directionality in drawing'.
14. E. B. Lehman and J. J. Goodnow 'Directionality in copying: memory, handedness and alignment effects', *Perceptual and Motor Skills*, 1975, *41*, 863-72.
15. C. Rice, 'Eye and hand movements in the training of perception', *Child Development*, 1931, *2*, 30-48.
16. F. L. Ilg and L. B. Ames, *School Readiness*.

17. R. S. Koenigsberg, 'An evaluation of visual *versus* sensorimotor methods for improving orientation discrimination of letter reversals by preschool children', *Child Development*, 1973, *44*, 764-9.
18. J. J. Goodnow and R. Levine, 'The grammar of action'.
19. E. R. and H. Lewis, 'An analysis of errors in the formation of manuscript letters by first grade children', *American Education Research Journal*, 1965, *2*, 25-35.
20. M. Bernbaum, 'Accuracy in children's copying'.
21. R. Serpell, 'Preferences for specific orientation of abstract shapes among Zambian children', *Journal of Cross-Cultural Psychology*, 1971, *21*, 225-39.
22. M. L. J. Abercrombie, R. L. Lindon and M. C. Tyson, 'Direction of drawing movements'.
23. L. G. Braine, 'Asymmetries of pattern perception'. 'Perceiving and copying the orientation of geometric shapes', *Journal o Research and Development in Education*, 1973, *6*, 44-55.

5. DEVELOPING CONVENTIONAL EQUIVALENTS (pp. 112-133)

1. B. Lloyd, *Perception and Cognition: a Cross-Cultural Perspective* (Harmondsworth: Penguin, 1972).
2. R. Arnheim, *Visual Thinking*.
   E. H. Gombrich, *Art and Illusion*.
3. F. E. Dart and P. L. Pradhan, 'The cross-cultural teaching of science', *Science*, 1967, *155*, 649-56.
4. J. Bamberger, 'Children's perception of rhythm in music', Massachusetts Institute of Technology, Report from Project Zero, 1971.
5. M. Stambak, 'Le probléme de rhythme dans le développement de l'enfant et dans les dyslexies de l'evolution', *Enfance*, 1951, *4*, 480-502.
6. J. J. Goodnow, 'Matching auditory and visual series: modality problem or translation problem?', *Child Development*, 1971, *42*, 1187-1201.

6. FROM OLD TO NEW EQUIVALENTS (pp. 134-149)

1. G. H. Luquet, *Les Dessins d'un Enfant* (Paris: Alcan, 1917). H. Eng. *The Psychology of Children's Drawings*.
2. R. Brown, 'The development of wh-questions in child speech', *Journal of Verbal Learning and Verbal Behaviour*, 1968, *7*, 279-90.

Suggested
further reading

RUDOLF ARNHEIM, *Art and Visual Perception* (Berkeley, Calif.: University of California Press, 2nd Edition, 1975).

An absorbing integration of analyses of art – produced by adults and children – with psychological studies of perception. In the author's words, the overall argument is that 'artistic activity is a form of reasoning in which perceiving and thinking are indivisibly intertwined'.

RUDOLF ARNHEIM, *Visual Thinking* (Berkeley, Calif.: University of California Press, 1971).

Why are the arts neglected in society and education? This book suggests that our culture tends to isolate the senses from thought, and to glorify words. If you read only three chapters, try Ch. 11 ('With feet on the ground'); Ch. 13 ('Words in their places'); and Ch.16 ('Vision in Education').

MARGARET CLARK, *Teaching Left-handed Children* (London: University of London Press, 1974).

A short, concise book that explodes many myths about the effect of left-handedness on learning to read, and offers helpful, specific advice on how to avoid difficulties in writing.

CAROL DONOGHUE, *The Development of Writing* (New York: Grossman (undated)).

One of the Jackdaw series, this is a small kit containing a brief history of writing plus illustrations of various scripts. This walk through time is a brief history of mankind, of interest for general reading and for presentation to any level of schoolchildren.

E. H. GOMBRICH, *Art and Illusion* (London: Phaidon, 1960).

This book contains no discussion of children's art, but provides a fascinating survey of various periods of art, linked to modern uses of signs and to discussions of what we mean by saying 'art' represents 'reality'.

RHODA KELLOGG, *Analyzing Children's Art* (Palo Alto, Calif: National Press, 1969).

A classic discussion of children's work, presenting a theory of stages and an insightful discussion of whether children's drawings should be used to measure 'intelligence'. For a much condensed version, see Rhoda Kellogg's article in *Psychology Today*, 1967, *1*, 16-25.

BETTY LARK-HOROVITZ, HILDA LEWIS, AND MARK LUCA, *Understanding Children's Art for Better Teaching* (Columbus, Ohio: Merrill, 1967).

Especially well-illustrated, with a straightforward account of trends in development. It does not contain the links to studies in perception and thought that other sources provide. It does, however, provide very useful suggestions on planning art activities and on helping children enjoy art.

KEVIN LYNCH, *The Image of the City* (Cambridge, Mass: Technology Press, 1960).

How can we study the way people perceive or 'map' the cities they live in? Lynch's book describes one way. It also contains an excellent final chapter discussing maps throughout the world and asking what the environmental conditions are that lead one to develop precise or 'fuzzy' maps.

Indexes

Subject Index

Index of Names

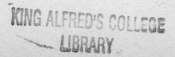

Fontana Paperbacks

Fontana is a leading paperback publisher of fiction and non-fiction, with authors ranging from Alistair MacLean, Agatha Christie and Desmond Bagley to Solzhenitsyn and Pasternak, from Gerald Durrell and Joy Adamson to the famous Modern Masters series.

In addition to a wide-ranging collection of internationally popular writers of fiction, Fontana also has an outstanding reputation for history, natural history, military history, psychology, psychiatry, politics, economics, religion and the social sciences.

All Fontana books are available at your bookshop or newsagent; or can be ordered direct. Just fill in the form and list the titles you want.